O9-AIG-355

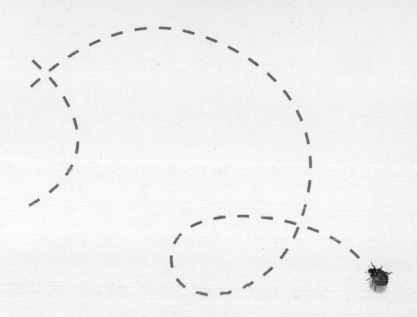

The Book of
Business Awesome

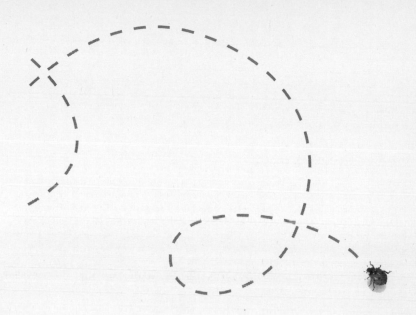

The Book of
Business Awesome

How Engaging Your Customers and Employees Can Make Your Business Thrive

Scott Stratten

Author of *UnMarketing*

WILEY

John Wiley & Sons, Inc.

Copyright © 2012 by Scott Stratten. All rights reserved

Published by John Wiley & Sons, Inc., Hoboken, New Jersey.
Published simultaneously in Canada.

No part of this publication may be reproduced, stored in a retrieval system, or transmitted in any form or by any means, electronic, mechanical, photocopying, recording, scanning, or otherwise, except as permitted under Section 107 or 108 of the 1976 United States Copyright Act, without either the prior written permission of the Publisher, or authorization through payment of the appropriate per-copy fee to the Copyright Clearance Center, Inc., 222 Rosewood Drive, Danvers, MA 01923, (978) 750-8400, fax (978) 646-8600, or on the web at www.copyright.com. Requests to the Publisher for permission should be addressed to the Permissions Department, John Wiley & Sons, Inc., 111 River Street, Hoboken, NJ 07030, (201) 748-6011, fax (201) 748-6008, or online at http://www.wiley.com/go/permissions.

Limit of Liability/Disclaimer of Warranty: While the publisher and author have used their best efforts in preparing this book, they make no representations or warranties with respect to the accuracy or completeness of the contents of this book and specifically disclaim any implied warranties of merchantability or fitness for a particular purpose. No warranty may be created or extended by sales representatives or written sales materials. The advice and strategies contained herein may not be suitable for your situation. You should consult with a professional where appropriate. Neither the publisher nor author shall be liable for any loss of profit or any other commercial damages, including but not limited to special, incidental, consequential, or other damages.

For general information on our other products and services or for technical support, please contact our Customer Care Department within the United States at (800) 762-2974, outside the United States at (317) 572-3993 or fax (317) 572-4002.

Wiley publishes in a variety of print and electronic formats and by print-on-demand. Some material included with standard print versions of this book may not be included in e-books or in print-on-demand. If this book refers to media such as a CD or DVD that is not included in the version you purchased, you may download this material at http://booksupport.wiley.com. For more information about Wiley products, visit www.wiley.com.

Library of Congress Cataloging-in-Publication Data:
Stratten, Scott.
    The Book of Business Awesome: How Engaging Your Customers and Employees Can Make Your Business Thrive / Scott Stratten.
    ISBN: 978-1-118-31522-4 (cloth)
    ISBN: 978-1-118-31545-3 (ebk)
    ISBN: 978-1-118-31546-0 (ebk)
    ISBN: 978-1-118-31547-7 (ebk)
    1. Relationship marketing. 2. Customer relations. 3. Management. I. Title.
HF5415.55
658.8'12–dc23
                                                                        2012010353

Printed in the United States of America
10 9 8 7 6 5 4 3

Contents

Awesome Acknowledgments

Inspired by "Here's to the Misfits" campaign for Apple.

HERE'S TO the misfits.

The entrepreneurs. The lone wolves in companies. The ones who believe businesses are built on relationships, not interruptions. To the ones who realize social is what social media is all about.

To the brave souls who would never cold-call or mislead just to gain a dollar. To the business start-ups who build their companies on the belief alone that they can do it.

The ones who realize that to have an awesome business you have to be awesome yourself.

This book is for you.

1

How One Man Changed a Billion-Dollar Brand

Every employee is your brand ambassador, your marketer, and the face of your company.

I WAS IN HARTFORD at the Hilton Garden Inn, on stop number eight of my 30-city UnBook Tour to promote *UnMarketing, Stop Marketing, Start Engaging*. The tour was amazing, but it also meant that I was living on airplanes and in hotels.

I rolled out of bed and headed downstairs for breakfast around 9:45 AM. Did I mention I'm not a morning person? It's actually one of the great problems I have in life: I love breakfast, and I hate mornings. The lobby had a breakfast buffet, and I'm not talking about the "continental" breakfast that most hotels throw in as a bonus with some Danish and something that resembles juice. This was a full spread of eggs, bacon, sausage, hash browns, cereal, bagels, you name it. I was pretty impressed with myself for being up in time for this feast, especially after crossing the continent the day before.

I told the chef that I'd like eggs, bacon, sausage, and hash browns (shut it, foodies); grabbed a juice; and took a seat. As soon as I sat down, I noticed they turned off the lights around the buffet. Score! I got there just in time.

Apparently not.

I dug in to my food, and it was bad. Old and cold. A bad combination for anything in life, let alone breakfast meats. I forced down some bacon, and after testing each of the other items, I couldn't continue. The waitress walked over with my bill and placed it on the table, without saying a word.

Most of the time in situations like these, what do we do? We take out our phones and share our bad experiences with the world, all the while quietly accepting them in real life. Most people would just allow this to happen and walk away, but I called her over. If I owned this business, I would want to know if something was up.

"Hi, the food was really bad. It was cold and old."

She just looked at me, not knowing what to do, and mentally took out the customer service playbook and said the "right" thing.

"I'll go get the manager."

And she walked away. I never asked for the manager or to have the bill taken care of. The manager came over and was nice and offered to have the chef make an omelet or something special for me. I declined, letting him know I really wasn't hungry anymore. I explained to him that I wasn't looking for a freebie but thought he needed to know. He picked up the bill and said they'd take care of it and apologized again.

This is where the customer service "apology" usually ends for 99.9 percent of businesses in the hospitality industry. Really, to be great at customer service, you need to be only mediocre, because everyone else sucks.

But not here.

The sous-chef, Forbes, ran out, stopped me from walking out, and looked shaken. Not in a shaken way like he'd been chewed out by anyone, but a sincere look of being upset. Did I mention he was about 6 foot 4 inches and 220 pounds? And that he ran at me? I have to admit, for a moment there, I regretted giving my feedback at all . . . .

He caught up to me and said, "Sir, I'm terribly sorry about your food this morning. A few things—although not excuses, we didn't know until we were cleaning up that the water underneath the food trays that keeps everything warm was gone, hence the food was cold. And I also should have never given you the food that was sitting out that long; I could have made you something fresh right there, but I thought you looked like you were in a hurry. Regardless, I'm terribly sorry; this is not how we operate, and we'd like another chance to make it up to you."

Wow.

This guy gave a damn that a guest had a subpar experience and he needed to make it right. We can't stop screwups, only how we remedy them. And the solution usually isn't hard. Most people who complain just want to feel validated, able to walk away feeling that someone has heard and understood them.

I didn't threaten to "tweet about it" or use "Do you know who I think I am?" I was just another person staying at the hotel. He could have simply talked about how much of a moron I was to his coworkers or brushed it off by saying, "You can't please everyone." He truly cared that they screwed up. He owned it. He changed my view of the Hilton Garden Inn and the Hilton overall. And he didn't have to.

To me, Forbes is the Hilton. Not their mission statement or logo. Every employee is your brand ambassador, your marketer, and the face of your company. Employees make a difference. Forbes made a difference for a billion–dollar hotel brand to me.

As I walked away and headed back up to my room he said, "I'd like to make this right."

And my reply was, "You already did."

2

Marketing Is a Verb

We need to hand off the branding baton to everyone in our company; everyone is a marketer.

WELCOME TO THE AWESOME side, fine reader. If you've chosen to start reading from this side of the book it's for one of three reasons:

1. You are the optimist, who sees the glass full because you just filled up the second half. You may or may not own a shirt with a unicorn on it.
2. You are the pessimist, so jaded by years in business that you are just hoping this side will give you hope and save your soul. You will last about three chapters before you switch over to the UnAwesome side, laughing diabolically . . . until you realize there is a part written about you in there. (By the way, the author fits here with you into Choice 2.)
3. You fall into the group thinking, "Wait! There's another side to this book!?!?" Or you bought this purely for the Awesome. Or you're my mom. Or you're reading this in the bookstore, and you

haven't even noticed the other side yet. You're waiting for the stock clerk to get you the latest *Twilight* novel, aren't you? Spoiler, he dies at the end.[1]

Whatever the reason, I'm glad you're here. To be awesome at business, you first have to realize that it can't be a policy. You can't mandate being awesome; you can't demand it. You have to hire awesome. You have to inspire awesome in others, and you have to be your awesome self. Awesome has to go through every level and every step of your company. Just like creating a great poster for a crappy movie doesn't make the movie any better; fantastic advertising for a horrible product won't change how people react once they use it. A known product name with a horrible return policy will hurt the original product. Every point of contact with your market is an opportunity to show them just how great your business really is.

Marketing is a verb. Awesome is a verb. You have to do it. People may come in because of great marketing, but they come back because of the experience. Loyalty isn't built through plastic cards; it's built through amazing experiences. No one ever said, "This restaurant was horrible, but did you see those ads in the paper!? We have to come back!!" It's our front lines that engage the market, and without them, our marketing means nothing. And sadly, although it is our front line, who have the first and most important contact with customers, they are often the lowest paid and least appreciated. We need to hand off the branding baton to everyone in our company; everyone is a marketer.

According to some really brilliant research about customer service by Nobel Prize winner Daniel Kahneman, as companies we should be focusing on the "Peak End Rule."[2] We judge our experiences with companies on the peak experience—either the worst or the best—and the end result. When people think about your business, they're going to focus on how good or how bad things got and on how everything worked out in the end. A really great salesperson who helps with an exchange can erase negative experiences along the way. The long wait in line and the bad music in your changing room are both forgotten.

---

[1] #TeamWesleySnipes, http://bit.ly/UnTwilight.
[2] http://onforb.es/PeakEndRule.

As long as you can out-awesome mistakes and resolve issues, customers will have a positive brand experience. Think about that.

We spend a great deal of time and energy focusing on what our competitors are doing when we should be working on improving ourselves, especially our front lines. We pour money into designing logos and brochures while we allow poor customer service to be the norm. We listen to statistics about when we should schedule our newsletter and ignore feedback from our employees. Did you know that, on average, a company saves more than $7,000 for each employee suggestion that is put into practice? These are the employees we value least, with the highest turnover. We brush them off, when we need to be handing them the brand baton.

In *The Book of Business Awesome*, we are going to look at how we can ensure we hand off the brand baton to every part of our business. We will look at how marketing, human resources, and public relations are all really under the same roof in business.

Some people will ask if this is another social media book. The way I see it, *social media* is simply another term for *communication*. Everything about business is communication. Whether you're trying to build brand awareness, improve customer service, or fill a vacancy, it's about people and their impact, good or bad, on our bottom line. So yes, this book is about people—what they say and what they do.

As you are reading, I want you to be thinking about how we can get better. Everyone is always jumping ahead to what's new, but I want us to make this the year of getting better at what we're already doing. We need to shed a few social pounds and stop trying to add more social media networks to our repertoire. Instead, let's get better where we already exist. Social media isn't about how many places you can be. It's about being amazing where you are.

3

Companies Aren't Awesome; People Are

We can't all be Zappos.com or work somewhere supercool like Google. And I'm glad that we can't, because if we were all the same, we'd all be perfectly ordinary.

WHEN WE SEE AWESOME COMPANIES at work around us, a few things can happen. As customers, we love them for it. They make the day-to-day chore of being a consumer so much more fun. We've all seen enough boring commercials. We actually spend time and money on ways to avoid being sold to, so the last thing we're looking for is another boring sales pitch. Let's be honest, we get excited as customers when we're just not treated badly. We can't help but lose our minds when something great happens.

As business owners, the effects are a little more complicated.

For me, seeing and reading about the great things people do in business makes me feel like I can do great things, too. That's why I love to share them. But sometimes, these examples can be intimidating and even limiting. It's very easy to see a company in action and think that you'll never be able to do the things it can do. Whether it's because you're just getting started, you don't have the same budget or resources, your industry isn't cool enough, or you're sure your customers wouldn't like it, other people's awesomeness can sometimes make us feel a little small.

Too often, feeling intimidated becomes our excuse not to be awesome.

I want to make sure that as you read this book you put yourself in the picture. Don't be overwhelmed or think that you need to mimic the stories I'm going to share. Instead, be inspired to find your own brand of awesome, that only you can bring to the table.

I know what you're thinking, and I want you to know you're absolutely right. We can't all be Zappos.com or work somewhere super cool like Google. And I'm glad that we can't, because if we were all the same, we'd all be perfectly ordinary. We spend too much time trying to be like others in business, when we should be focusing on finding our own story. I promise you, we all can find our window of awesome in our job and our companies and great things can happen. That's what this book is all about.

So how do we keep ourselves from being intimidated or overwhelmed? Business is built on relationships—on the simple act of people interacting and engaging with others. And that all starts with the individual, with you. In every great business story there is an individual who started it all. Every great marketing campaign started with someone deciding to take a chance and step outside the norm. The outstanding customer service a company is known for was executed one contact at a time and started with one voice deciding to care. They may not have always executed it on their own. But at the start there was one.

I call this *situational awesome*, and we can all do it. We have access to it every day—in our attitudes and in our interactions. It starts with the passion we have for our work and our product. It can be as simple as just giving a damn about our customers. Sometimes it's the smile we give across a store counter to someone looking for a little help. It might sound simple, but this is the start of every great story I share in this book. Someone decided to care or to try. This can be a cashier at a pet store, a janitor, or a volunteer.

Next we have *occupational awesome*, which although similar to situational awesome, comes with a little more definition.

Occupational awesome is about our roles and how they define windows of awesome for us. For example, customer service agents have a special opportunity to make amazing things happen in their companies every day. As we will speak about often in the chapters ahead, frontline workers, especially, are capable of making a huge impact on brand perception, because their jobs give them so many opportunities to engage with customers.

Other positions in a company come with their own opportunities. Although it might be easy to assume that more senior positions would have an easier time finding opportunities for awesome, this isn't always true. Every single job in a company is important, and every single person a part of your branding and marketing.

Next up, we have *divisional awesome*. This is all about groups and the amazing things that can happen when people come together and the results are truly greater than the sum of their parts. Here we also start to see the opportunity for situational or occupational awesome to start spreading throughout a company. This is where one person's passion can start to shape an entire company. And when one division of a company starts to shine, it's hard for the others to ignore.

And last, but certainly not least, is *institutional awesome*. This is where you find companies that, through the work of individuals and groups, have created brand-wide amazingness. These are the companies known for their outstanding customer service, products, services, and campaigns.

This level has an especially powerful role to play, through hiring and human resources. Here, a company can create opportunities for awesome at every level, from the individual up. At the institutional level we also see what public relations (PR) can do for a brand and how awesome PR will not only do damage control but will make the company come out looking even better than it did before the mistake.

Together, all these levels become your brand voice, the message, and the image people think of when they think about your company. No matter whether your business is a one-person show just getting started or a multinational corporation, whether you are a frontline worker or a top-level executive, you can create awesome. The individual is the start.

How are you going to be awesome today?[1]

---

[1]Scratch that. You're reading this book, which makes you already awesome by default. High-five.

4

Remarry Your Current Customers

Push those beds back together and start treating them the way they deserve. This is how we create ecstatic customers.

MOST OF THE TIME, we focus our sales and marketing on acquiring new customers—even though it's a well-known fact in business (as stated in many fancy studies I've never read) that it costs *waaay* more to acquire new customers than keep your current ones. Above and beyond the greater cost, when we lose customers, we also lose the opportunity for word-of-mouth, one of the most valuable ways of marketing we have. We should be working harder to take our customers from static to ecstatic, to get their mouths moving, sharing great experiences they've had with our company.

We treat our current customers as though we've been married to them for 47 years—and the past 46 weren't so great. We're not even talking to them at breakfast. I want us to court them and remarry our current customers. Push those beds back together and start treating them the way they deserve. This is how we create ecstatic customers.

When I went to my bank a few months ago, I saw that they were offering new iPods to anyone who opened a new account. Sweet, right? I like iPods. I've been with the bank for more than 20 years, and when I asked them if I could get a new iPod, they said, "We're sorry; it's only for new accounts." To get this incentive, I literally had to close my accounts, end my business, and start off new. That's no way to treat a loyal customer.

Cell phone companies are notorious for this practice. After completing what seemed like a 57-year agreement for my BlackBerry, I was excited to hear I'd earned an upgrade. However, when I looked into it a little further, all my "upgrade" meant was that I could get a new phone and renew the same long-term contract I had already been using. There was no incentive for loyalty, no reward for the roughly $15,000 I had spent over the duration of my contract. I was treated exactly the same as any new customer who had wandered through their doors that day, and it didn't exactly leave me feeling warm and fuzzy.

We are losing customers in the name of getting new bright and shiny ones.

According to the Harris Interactive, Customer Experience Impact Report, 89 percent of consumers report that they quit doing business with a company because of a bad customer experience, up from 59 percent four years ago.[1] That's a number you cannot ignore in the name of finding new customers, and it is growing fast. Social media and smartphones mean people are sharing their customer service experiences like never before. We have more and more options at our fingertips. So when your service sucks, I can find your competitors in one click. Or even better, if they're smart, when I complain about your brand online, they will find me.

We are losing our customers because of poor service. We need to stop this trend and start working hard to keep our current customers happy. The people on the front line who are responsible for customer experience, from first impressions to handling complaints, are our least paid and most underappreciated. The fact that these important people are undervalued shows through in how our customers experience our

---

[1] *Source*: Harris Interactive, Customer Experience Impact Report. http://bit.ly/CSEIR. Right Now, Headquarters in Bozeman, Montana. 2011.

company. Good hiring, providing training, and creating a culture of value for our front line is our best marketing tool.

In the next few chapters, we're going to review some customer service case studies, both in person and online. We'll look at the ways social media can be an amazing tool for social and publicized customer service, and we'll examine new ways to bring more awesome into our businesses. For updates to customer service stories and for new examples of awesome, visit www.TheBookOfBusinessAwesome.com/CustomerService.

5

The Sun Rises Online

If fans are sharing their love for your event, product, or service, you should be taking advantage of these ecstatic, rabid fans to let others know just how awesome you are.

IT'S NO SECRET to those who know me that I'm a sports freak. And one of the benefits of all the travelling I do is having the opportunity to see sporting events in different cities all over the world. During the UnBook Tour for the first book, I was able to take part in the Sport Addicts Trifecta in Boston, seeing a Celtics, Bruins, and Red Sox game all within four days.

One of the coolest things for me at sporting events is checking out how each team uses social media. I end up paying a lot of attention to how each team manages their brand online and engages with fans in real time during events. What could be better than bringing together sports and social media, two of my favorite things? As expected, what I find is a whole lot of variety, with some teams really embracing social media while others completely ignore it.

14

When I was in Phoenix, I really wanted to see a Coyotes hockey game and a Suns basketball game. I checked my schedule and their schedules; everything worked, so I went online and bought tickets on Ticketmaster. I didn't go in expecting to have any kind of social media experience. I bought a ticket the same day and was able to score a seat in the first row of the upper level, which is a great spot to watch a basketball game, or any sport for that matter. I was really excited about the spot, which made me somewhat curious as to how I was able to get such a good seat the same day as the game. I figured it was just luck and didn't think anymore about it. Then I headed off to the game.

I had heard a lot about the Phoenix Suns and how they had embraced social media in a great way. I had never actually connected with anybody from the team before deciding to go to the game. I didn't tweet to them beforehand, didn't tell them I'm kind of a big deal on a fairly irrelevant social media site that falsely inflates my ego, and ask for a free ticket. I paid my own way. I don't like to leverage my artificial clout for free things,[1] so the Suns didn't know I was going to be there.

I arrived at the game and sat down in my seat, realizing very quickly why it had been available at such short notice—there was a pole right in the center of my field of view. I couldn't see half the basketball court. I had to sit awkwardly, leaning into the aisle, to see anything.

What would you do? Usually, when I'm not happy with an experience as a customer, I let the company have a chance in person to make it better. But in this case, not knowing the arena, and feeling pretty lazy after the trip there, there was no way I was going to get up and hunt down customer service—especially since I knew that if I did find someone, they would most likely point out the disclaimer on the back of my ticket and do nothing for me at all. But I still wanted to give the Suns a chance, so I did the next best thing I could think of and sent out a tweet.

I added the Phoenix Suns account name to it so that they would have the chance to catch it and waited to see what they would do, if anything at all.

Please understand, I wasn't happy but I also wasn't upset enough to storm out and demand my money back. I was a static customer, they had my purchase, and I had chosen them and given them my

---

[1]But I'm more than happy to accept any of the free things you want to send me, so let me know.

business. I would have watched the game and left, having a mediocre experience. This is where most customers sit, in static mode. They are just there, not overly pleased, not overly angry. They just exist. Letting them sit there is the wrong mentality for brands to take. We shouldn't be looking at how many customers we have but at how many *ecstatic* customers we have. Static customers come and go very easily, not angry enough to tell you why they're upset—and not happy enough to have any loyalty. When we do things to shift them into being ecstatic, loyalty increases. Ecstatic customers are also more willing to tell you when they become upset, giving you an opportunity to keep them from leaving. Instead of a revolving door of static customers, create ecstatic ones and they'll bring people in the door for you.

Back to the Suns game . . . . Next thing I knew, less than 10 minutes after my tweet, the Phoenix Suns account tweeted back! They were listening! They asked me to please DM them my seat location and told me someone would be right there to fix everything. Sure enough, Vice President of Digital, Jeramie McPeek himself, came to my seat and escorted me down to the Phoenix Suns luxury suite, from where I watched the rest of the game. Before you get your manties in a bunch and say they treated me this way only because of my large following online, I was not the only one in the suite. There were seven other people from Twitter there. It was a special promotion, where they were upgrading random fans who were using Twitter. After the game, they had a Twitter press conference for fans to come and ask the president of the team questions. The Suns showed me that they really understood one thing about business online: social media isn't a campaign; it's a way of business. Social media is an extension of business.

Why wouldn't you want to listen? If fans are sharing their love for your event, product, or service, you should be taking advantage of these ecstatic, rabid fans to let others know just how awesome you are. A simple reply letting fans know how much you appreciate them can make a world of difference. Of course, I understand that this can be hard to manage, but look at the value that can come out of it. Answering the phone every time someone calls is hard to manage, too, isn't it? But we understand that we need to get people on the other end of those calls and make our customer's experience as good as possible. A tweet is no different, except this time when we make things right, it's public and it's social.

6

Sporting Event Awesome

Social media isn't just talking sometimes. It's reducing the barrier between company and consumer and between people— opening up opportunities for awesome.

WHEN I'M ON STAGE, I ask the audience to leave their phones on. I want them to tweet about the talk. I want them to make everyone who isn't there in the room with us jealous. At the same time, it's my job to hold their attention. I want them to constantly be in this state of distress—between wanting to share the awesome stuff coming from stage and not wanting to miss anything while they type. I think that should be the goal of every live event. If what is happening on stage isn't engaging enough to keep your audience from playing games on their phones, that's really your problem, not theirs.

When done right, not only can fans share how awesome they think an event is, but they can add to the event. A perfect example of a fan adding to a sport by using Twitter is the story of Julia Probst, a German soccer fan who is deaf. During games, she reads the lips of players and coaches and shares what she sees online with her followers.

I love this story because she uses Twitter to both share her experience and add to the game she loves. One of her followers brilliantly pointed out that by reading lips, she actually is taking in parts of the event we can't—that she is not the one who cannot hear; we are. She's raising awareness for the deaf online in one of the most awesome ways I've ever seen. It is such a cool use of her skill combined with technology. I only wish I could speak a little German so that I could understand what she's tweeting. You should check her out here: www.twitter.com/EinAugenschmaus.

We talk a lot about human resources (HR) and hiring coming up later on in the book. I can't stress enough that marketing, HR, public relations, sales, and customer service are really all seen as one by your market. Usually we focus on the negative side, driving home that what you tweet may keep you from getting a job or cause you to lose the one you have, but in the case of Jerry Rizzo, tweeting landed him the job offer of his dreams.

Jerry was a longtime fan of the 76ers[1] and a social media addict. The team was running a contest to choose its new mascot, and Jerry and one of his friends noticed that neither of the finalists, one Phil E. Moose and a B. Franklin Dogg, had a Twitter account. So the duo took it upon themselves to open the accounts and began tweeting on their behalves. In very little time, the accounts had a number of followers and were adding to the fan excitement about the contest.

The accounts quickly gained fans and the attention of the team. At first, there was some dispute as to whether Jerry had stepped over the line and who could really claim ownership for the accounts. In the end, Jerry was rewarded beyond what even he could have hoped for. Jerry and the friend he was working with on the accounts were given box seats and season tickets.[2] In the end, 76er CEO Adam Aron was so impressed by their creativity and hard work that Jerry was offered a job as the official social media coordinator for the team.[3]

How's that for some Twitter ROI (return on investment) right there? I love this example of how a fan saw a window of awesome opportunity open and jumped right in. He showed personality, a

---

[1] Which is enough to give him my sympathy.
[2] http://on.mash.to/76ersMascot.
[3] http://yhoo.it/TwitterMascot.

love of the team and game, and took a fun idea and turned it into an opportunity. That's what social media should be—just another opportunity to show the world how awesome you are. If you want to check out the mascot accounts, visit www.twitter.com/PhilEMoose and www.twitter.com/BFranklinDogg.

Sometimes the person being awesome isn't a fan but one of the athletes themselves. During the 2011 NBA lockout, Oklahoma City Thunder player Kevin Durant used Twitter to stay connected with fans and show he was sharing in their boredom. On October 31, he sent out the tweet shown in Figure 6.1, looking for something to do.

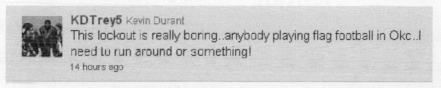

KDTrey5 Kevin Durant
This lockout is really boring..anybody playing flag football in Okc..I need to run around or something!
14 hours ago

Figure 6.1   from @KDTrey5

A student from Oklahoma State replied to him, never expecting to hear anything back, and invited Kevin to join in on a fraternity flag football game later that night. Durant showed up and scored four touchdowns.

How awesome is that?! I love how social media can remind us how we're all just people, no matter what we do for a living or where we live. This tweet was one person talking to others, sharing his experience, and it ended up with a really cool result. If you want to check out Kevin Durant on Twitter, this is where you can find him: www.twitter.com/KDTrey5.

Just with these few examples, we can see that social media isn't just talking sometimes. It's reducing the barrier between company and consumer and between people—opening up opportunities for awesome. We just have to be willing to take them. That's why it's wrong to put down chatting online about regular stuff. Real life isn't epic. We connect over the day-to-day things that make us all human. Whether we are famous athletes or fans, social media is a place where we can get to know one another and connect. And I think that's awesome.

7

I Think Geeks Rule

Your online front line, the people who are e-mailed and chatted with every day about problems, can save your brand and reputation on a daily basis.

A HUGE AMOUNT of customer service is now done online, through e-mail or chat. I don't know about you, but I'm a big fan of anything that helps me talk on the phone less. When I have a question or problem to share with a company I've done business with, I would much rather deal with the issue online using e-mail or chat than try to deal with it offline.

When customers connect with you virtually about a complaint, the initial problem is almost always minor; maybe something has been broken during shipping, or they didn't get the right software with their download link. A small issue has happened, and customers are looking for some kind of empathy—just to be heard. As customers, we are very forgiving and understanding when businesses own up to what they have done wrong. As a society, we don't expect perfection. We simply want someone to apologize and at the very least have the company own the problem.

You might think that virtual customer service gives us less opportunity for engagement and issue resolution, but that isn't true. We open up a new way for customers to communicate with us—giving them more choices, no longer forcing people to use the phone or come in for assistance. E-mails can be easily forwarded to the correct person in our company to properly answer questions. Online customer service can be simple and easy to use, with few hoops for our customers to jump through—which means there is a lot of room to be awesome.

One example of a site that's using online chat for customer service really well is ThinkGeek.com. I love the site, a place where I've purchased many unnecessary items I love. Have a look at the chat that follows.

Customer Service Online Chat

Mary: Hiya Kyler!

Mary: Er, Kyle!

Mary: What can I do for you this fine evening?

That works too: That works too!

That works too: . . . oh now my name is that. Wonderful.

Mary: HA!

That works too: Anyways . . . My problems is that I made an order but did not set up an account during the order.

Mary: No worries, EVERYONE does that

That works too: And one of the products was damaged upon receipt :'(

Mary: And you're anting your shiny GeekPoints?

That works too: According to the FAQ I need to press the "return" link

Mary: OH NO

(continued)

(*continued*)

Mary: Okay, I can fix that, one moment

That works too: Thanks!

Mary: which item was damaged?

That works too: The whirlybird :(I mean, Gyro copter

That works too: Landing strut plastic piece is snapped off.

Mary: Not the HELI!

That works too: I know! But I can still terrorize my cats in the meantime with my laser pointer.

Mary: Please do

Mary: And take video to share with the internets

Mary: because that is ALWAYS hilarious

That works too: Can't go wrong with that.

Mary: So, I'm going to send you a new helicopter

Mary: And you can go ahead and keep the old one for parts

That works too: That's awesome!

Mary: The rotor blades are always handy to have around

That works too: Mary, you are a queen among . . . queens

That works too: I think that's how that goes.

Mary: I'll take that!

Mary: *Chuckles*

Mary: So keep an eye on your doorstep for the new heli

Mary: And we should email you when it ships too

That works too: I will! Thank you very much for keeping my nerdhopes alive

Mary: It's what I do!

Source: http://i.imgur.com/TaZDN.jpg. © 2011 Think Geek, Inc. Used with permission.

When was the last time you read a customer service story that made you smile like you are now?

As you can see, this is a loyal customer who had purchased something and then had a little problem. A single customer service representative, with a great personality, some attitude, and empathy totally turned his experience around. ThinkGeek.com might be a website with a ton of staff, who have marketing plans and branding campaigns, but in the end, this single agent is their company. She is their brand.

Your online front line, the people who are e-mailed and chatted with every day about problems, can save your brand and reputation on a daily basis. There is no other department in a company that can say that. Customer service is the extension of your brand past the point of purchase. And just because it is digital, does not mean it can't be awesome.

8

DKNY 4 U 2

Why not use social customer service?

WHEN I SHARE THE AWESOME STORIES I have of personal interactions with brands and companies online, I often get this reply: "Well, of course they were nice to you. You are kind of a big deal. You wrote a book about customer service . . . ."

When Dustin Godsey wrote a post about his interaction with the brand DKNY, he titled it "I'm Not a Superstar . . . DKNY Just Treated Me Like One."[1] He explains that he isn't a CEO, or a social media all-star with thousands of followers. To him, this means that when a company gives him great customer service, they aren't doing it expecting a social media windfall or a ton of exposure. Whether we like to admit it or not, we are all a lot nicer, more careful, and more conscientious in business when we think people are watching.

Dustin had purchased a DKNY shirt, and when ironing it one morning, he found a tear in the cuff. So, like many of us do, he tweeted

---

[1] http://bit.ly/DKNYisAwesome.

@dgodz
Dustin Godsey

Looks like I've got a trip to the
tailor to make. Wear a shirt twice
& the cuff starts to fall off? Not
cool, @dkny.
pic.twitter.com/klLOfsDG

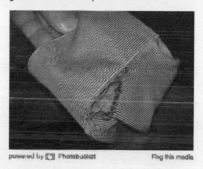

powered by [ ] Photobucket   Flag this media

Figure 8.1   Tweet from @dgodz

a complaint—a passive one really. He included the Twitter handle
@DKNY, without even confirming the account name to see if they
were active or even present. He says that he was just upset to be
missing his favorite shirt and tweeted about it, not expecting a reply.
His tweet is shown in Figure 8.1.

Ten minutes later, at 9:17 on a Sunday night, he received a reply
from @DKNY asking him to DM his information to them. They didn't
ask for proof of purchase or reply about what they couldn't do. They
didn't give an excuse. It turned out that Dustin had purchased the shirt
from an outlet mall, which many companies would use as an excuse to
not stand behind their product—but not DKNY. They simply asked
Dustin to let them know if he would prefer a replacement of his original
shirt, if they could find it in stock, or another of their shirts in his size.

And a few days later, Dustin had a new shirt and DKNY set a
new standard of customer service for him. The thing is, because their
customer service was social, the experience reached much further than
Dustin and his shirt. DKNY did a lot of things right.

- **They were listening**. If he had called the complaint into their
  customer service line, we would expect them to answer, so why do

we all expect the tweet to go without a reply? He included their account in the tweet, but without looking it up to confirm, he really didn't mean it as a direct communication to them. He was venting, as we all do online about something that bugged him. The value of this passive conversation is overwhelming and untapped. If you aren't already listening to what people are saying about your brand online, you need to start.

Brands spend countless dollars on focus groups when customer feedback is already being given out in the open, just waiting for you to pay attention and hear it. It can be as simple as setting up a keyword search on Twitter or a Google Alert or using a listening tool such as Radian6, Vocus, or Trackur. I recommend searching for your own brand name and industry keywords.

- **They owned the issue.** DKNY did not argue with Dustin about his shirt. All too often, our first reaction is to be defensive when something goes wrong, but it shouldn't be. People don't want an argument. They want to be heard. Think about the end experience. What will we remember about this brand? Not the torn shirt or the complaint. We will remember the amazing service and the result—a new shirt for Dustin.
- **They did it all online.** Why not use social customer service? Dustin's followers saw the interaction. His followers shared it with their followers. His blog readers saw it. Fans of the brand saw it. Haters, too. They took what would have been a private conversation (that may never have even happened if Dustin hadn't wanted to call in his complaint) and turned it into awesome. Public, shared awesome.

As we see here, they took a common product problem and turned it into an awesome brand experience, transforming Dustin from a static customer into an ecstatic brand loyalist, just because they were listening. They did not take his business for granted because he had already made a purchase, and their actions set a new standard for customer service online. This story put the brand on my radar and changed a clothing company into a clothing company that cares.

9

PR Stands for People React

Timing. Accountability. Appropriate personality.

No OTHER INDUSTRY or discipline has been affected by the ramifications of social media and online engagement more than public relations (PR). Classically, PR was all about getting the word out, and social media has changed that in a number of ways. More and more, PR is about getting the word back in and managing online engagement gone very wrong.

Everything from rogue employees who trip up to bad press or reviews about your brand will spread like wildfire across the social media tubes. Bad customer service or negative reactions to an ad campaign or product are shared online every day. It's one of the reasons companies shy away from social media. But what they don't understand is that this is exactly why they and their PR people need to be there.

Individuals now have a voice, and when they share negative brand experiences with friends and followers, PR is often called upon to fix it. If your greatest asset as a PR person is who you can fax things to, then you are about 20 years behind. You need to learn the world of social media.

PR no longer stands for only public relations; it means people react, people respond, and people reach out.

As an industry, PR should be very excited about new ways of communicating and marketing in business. Social media is public relations, brands engaging with the public. It should be the backbone, the default, and a no-brainer when it comes to PR. Yet PR departments are resisting it, feeling threatened and concerned about losing control of their message—the voice, story, and communication from brands to the public. As companies, we dream of having writers and reporters tell our stories, but the most valuable voices already are. They are talking about your industry, business, or product each and every day.

To be awesome in business means we have to be awesome at PR, even though we may no longer be able to create and craft stories the way we could before social media, handing them out to reporters and journalists. The messages are now authentic and driven by personal experiences. The power of these stories when they are positive is brand magic. We read that some of our trusted friends love something, and we want to try it. We learn to trust it.

But when those messages are negative, the results can be disastrous for a company. Fortunately, they don't have to be, and PR is what makes all the difference. Awesome PR in the face of a social media disaster can turn it all around, making the brand look better after the mistake than it did before.

In the next few chapters, we're going to look at the clusterfarks that happen in social media and how awesome PR turned them all around by making us see these mistakes as human.

What makes the difference between a PR fail and a PR success?

1. **Timing:** The speed at which information, and public reaction, can travel and grow today is exponentially faster than it was just five years ago. Waiting to respond to an event for days can equal virtual light-years online. Most of the successful PR responses I have witnessed happened immediately, and never more than within a few hours. The highest rate of reaction and engagement to a tweet is within the first few minutes. When the reactions begin to swell,

the online world is up and doing its research. These hours are the window that makes the difference between a Huffington Post blog about your marketing nightmare versus the one about your awesome PR recovery.

2. **Accountability:** Own it. We forgive, but brands are so scared of owning a problem that they forget the basic childhood lesson; tell the truth and say you're sorry like you mean it. None of the great PR examples swept their problem under the rug. They allowed the problem to enhance their dedication to a resolution.

3. **Appropriate personality:** Depending on the severity of the problem, showing some lighthearted personality can help the cause. We all trip up sometimes, and not all mistakes online are better managed heavy-handedly. On the other hand, when the issue is severe, treat it as such. Remember the key to making it personal is being appropriate. This means being respectful of those affected and the issue at hand. Treating an issue in need of a PR recovery with ill-timed humor or insensitivity will do nothing but make things dramatically worse.

These three ingredients create a great recipe for potentially turning a bad situation into a more positive one. As you read through these examples, think about the ways in which you handle mistakes that arise in your business and how you can turn them around. When it hits the fan in business, it's not time to hide behind the fan. It's time to be awesome. I want you to fan the flames. Instead of putting out fires, stoke them. Make them burn brighter. Make every mistake an opportunity. Fan the flames with so much awesome that it is 10 times brighter than the original spark that started the problem. Stop trying to be proactive; we need to learn how to react better.

For updates and more examples of awesome PR, visit www .TheBookOfBusinessAwesome.com/PublicRelations.

10

The Red Cross Is Getting Slizzerd

They chose to make their reaction louder than the mistake and in the end came out looking better than before it happened.

WHEN YOU TWEET for the most recognized brand in the world and you mess up, people notice. You know that time you accidentally sent a DM as a tweet and freaked out, rushing back in to delete it, thankful that only about three people caught it? That doesn't work for an international organization. People see. They take screenshots.[1] And they react. Deleting isn't going to help; something needs to be done about it.

Most of the time, accounts delete and apologize. They explain they were wrong, misinformed, or perhaps even hacked. The original comment is removed, and the company works hard to make people forget and move on. Depending on how emotive the post, and who you've managed to offend, this may or may not work. The thing is, online, what you say can live forever. I think instead of running from

---

[1]Some of them even put it into books. Jerks.

Figure 10.1   Tweet from @RedCross #1

these mistakes, we should face them and use them as an opportunity to be great.

The tweet shown in Figure 10.1 was sent out by mistake under the Red Cross account. The woman managing the Red Cross's Twitter presence was using an app on her phone that allowed her to tweet from multiple accounts, and the rogue tweet was meant to come from her own personal account.

So what would you do if you sent something like this out on behalf of your brand, other than change your pants of course?

Would you:

- Delete the rogue tweet and pray nobody saw it?
- Apologize for the tweet, fire the person who sent it, and send out a press release?
- Decide to be awesome and tweet something shortly after, like the Red Cross did (see Figure 10.2)?

How awesome is that? This is my very favorite example of a brand recovery. I show it during my talks to audiences around the world. You would be hard-pressed to find a bigger or more conservative brand out there than the Red Cross. Yet they had one of the best, and funniest, recoveries I have ever seen to a tweet gone wrong. So much so that, as rarely happens, the apology traveled further online than the initial

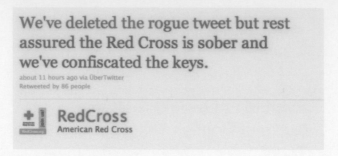

We've deleted the rogue tweet but rest assured the Red Cross is sober and we've confiscated the keys.

about 11 hours ago via ÜberTwitter
Retweeted by 86 people

RedCross
American Red Cross

Figure 10.2   Tweet from @RedCross #2. Bring on the Awesome!

incident. Dogfish Brewery saw the tweet, and the fallout, and decided to support a blood drive the following day. Turning something that could have gone wrong into something amazing. No hardline apology or public firing could ever have resulted in the same outcome. Their reaction matched the nature of the mistake perfectly.

The Red Cross's decision to react to the tweet was simple and funny. It matched the nature of the mistake very well. Wendy Harman, director of social media for the American Red Cross, wrote about the story.[2] This is one of my favorite excerpts, and a brilliant explanation of how to respond to social media missteps:

> After all, this wasn't a purposeful message gone wrong and it wasn't about the mission of our organization. Our Twitter account just tripped on the sidewalk, and instead of throwing a temper tantrum about tripping, we acted like any self-aware person would: we dusted ourselves off, looked around to acknowledge the trip with those who caught it, and had a chuckle with them.

Isn't that a brilliant explanation? "Our Twitter account just tripped...." Being able to put your mistakes in business into perspective is a rare and awesome thing. We speak a lot about companies not reacting, or reacting too slowly or not effectively, but there is also a danger in overreacting online. As we see with the Red Cross, it's the ability to match our fix to the nature of a mistake that can make all the difference.

---

[2]http://bit.ly/RedCrossPR.

When the Red Cross's reply went up, they didn't just go back to bed. The brand was committed to the conversation and stayed up all night to respond to feedback. They understood that the nature of social media would require Wendy to be there, present and ready to respond actively. Caring enough about people's reactions shows so much about her understanding of how this event needed to be managed.

Now, I never saw the initial tweet. I didn't know that the Red Cross made a mistake. They chose to make their reaction louder than the mistake and in the end came out looking better than before it happened. Immediate. Accountable. Personality. This is a perfect example of all three in motion and how they can take a rogue tweet and turn it into brand magic.

11

Grand Rapids Serves Up Some Humble Pie

When someone slings mud at your brand, you can either throw mud back, or you can rise above it and throw some "American Pie."

WHAT HAPPENS WHEN THE PROBLEM isn't something your brand has done but the perception of what it is? Lists of popular and unpopular destinations in travel have always been extremely influential to the public. How would you react if you were on one of the worst lists of all time? Negative feedback and ratings are always hard to take, but how you decide to react can be an opportunity.

When *Newsweek*'s website named Grand Rapids, Michigan, a dying city, Rob Bliss decided it was time to be awesome. He created "Grand Rapids LipDub," an amazing nine-minute-long video, set to a live recording of "American Pie"; it included thousands of people singing and taking part in what seems like a spontaneous walk through their town. The video is brilliant and seamless, which is especially amazing since Rob had never made a video before.

Once he had the video planned out, it was divided into 26 scenes, which they rehearsed the week before. Truly a community project, the city shut down the streets for the shoot and they raised $40,000 in sponsorships from local businesses to pay for production.

Bliss wrote and directed video, and it was shot in one take. It's full of energy and fun, exactly the opposite of what a dying city would be like. As of the day I wrote this chapter, the video had been viewed more than 4.5 million times. Roger Ebert called it "the best music video ever made." Take that, *Newsweek*!

There are many examples of lipdubs out there. The first one I ever saw was back in 2007, to "Flagpole Sitta" by Harvey Danger. The company who created it was called Connected Ventures.[1] Since then I have seen them for everything from campus recruitment to old-age homes. They are not easy to put together; they have to be really well done to be awesome.

The Grand Rapids one stood out because of how positive it was, as a reaction to such a negative critique. Instead of the city penning a biting letter to the editor about how their city isn't dying, they showed it. Awesome like this doesn't have an expiry date; it is evergreen. It will live on online, gaining new views and fans for the city every day. This is one of the reasons branding and rebranding are so effective online. Everyday people search "Grand Rapids" and find their awesome video. If you scan the code below, you can watch, too. You really should; I promise it will make you smile. You can also see the video at http://bit.ly/GrandRapidsVid.

When someone slings mud at your brand, you can either throw mud back, or you can rise above it and throw some "American Pie."

---

[1]http://bit.ly/LipdubAwesome.

12

The One Thing More Delicious Than Ice Cream

When you do awesome things, it makes people want to share the awesome.

THERE ARE COUNTLESS BLOG POSTS ONLINE about how out of touch PR people are when they try to reach out to influential bloggers and social media types. From mass-e-mailed blind press releases to not understanding how social media really works.

I finally have a story about the opposite. I was already working with the brand when it happened. Magnum Ice Cream had hired me as a spokesperson, and I got an awesome compensation package to be part of their campaign. Seriously, cash and ice cream. Cash. Ice cream. Yeah . . . amazing.

I was approached to work with Magnum by Duri Al Ajrami, who at the time was director of social marketing/senior partner at OgilvyOne Canada. We had worked together before, and I have always been so impressed with his ability to connect his clients and us—the crazy social media/blogger entitlement types about a campaign. As the beloved go-between, Duri is the best. He does his research and understands the process.

Duri dropped me an e-mail and explained that Magnum Ice Cream was launching in Canada and they wanted me on board. I'd hoped it was because of my rugged good looks and boyish charm, but it turns out it was mainly because I have a platform. In my first book I wrote about platforming, and how you can build your online voice. Think of a platform like a stage you stand on, with an audience to match. Clients want to work with people in social media because they want access to this stage, to reach your followers. Duri's job was to find the right fit between his client, Magnum, and a platform, and he knew I had the right one.

He said all the right things: I had to tweet and blog only if I wanted to and talk about it only when and if I wanted to. He knew I wasn't going to post a blog on UnMarketing as a "sponsored" post to say how yummy their ice cream is. We high-fived, they shipped me a case of ice cream in dry ice, I ate most of it in a two-day binge, I then reflected on what went so wrong in my life that made me eat a case of ice cream in 48 hours, and finally I decided to record a video.

The video was me talking about how much I loved the double chocolate ice cream bars they had sent me, as well as my need to point out false advertising: there were, in fact, four kinds of chocolate. This, of course, would make them quad chocolate ice cream bars. You can watch the video that I uploaded to their facebook page at http://bit.ly/AwesomePR.

I thought it was a fun way to talk about it! I even titled it "Magnum's False Advertising," which I'm sure made the client throw up a little. I talked about how the box said the flavor was "Double Chocolate" even though there are actually four layers of chocolate, and I demanded it be changed to "Quad Chocolate." I enjoyed making it because I was my smart-ass self. Duri loved it, and my friends liked it, too. Those living outside of Canada also enjoyed it, even though the contest was open only to Canadians. Perfect. All's good, everyone's happy, let's go home and eat ice cream.

Think again.

A few days later, Duri just showed up at my house (he e-mailed first; relax) and said, "I have a gift for you!" Figure 12.1 shows what he handed me.

Figure 12.1   My very own ice cream!

Are. You. Kidding. Me?!?! If you didn't catch it, look at it again.

They loved the video so much, they "whipped up" four custom boxes of the ice cream with my new flavor description. And these aren't stickers slapped on; it's four real boxes, with the ice cream bars inside. Talk about immediacy! They didn't table the idea for their next brand awareness meeting or set up a committee to decide how to react to my video. Someone had an idea and ran with it.

I literally lost it in the driveway, ran upstairs, and typed up a second blog post—right away. On my blog, the same place where I had decided previously not to write about it in the first place.

Just because you're in an agency, doesn't mean you can't be awesome. You can still find personality and awesome for the brands you represent.

The blog was read by 18,000 people. The contest had a huge effect on the number of online conversations taking place about Magnum and how they compared with other ice cream companies. Everyone was talking about the contest—which is exactly the kind of buzz Magnum was looking for. Have a look at the graph shown in Figure 12.2.

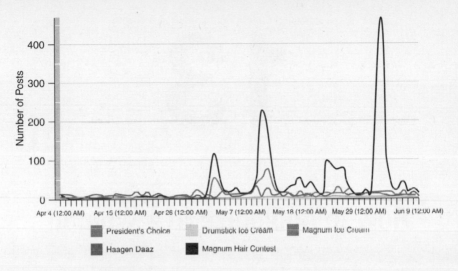

Figure 12.2   Magnum buzz

The highest spike in mentions that you see was on June 1, when my custom Quad Chocolate bars post went out. OgilvyOne's data on the campaign show that the number one buzzword during that time was "Awesome." My word, of course. During the first month of the campaign, there were more than 3,000 mentions of the contest and Magnum Ice Cream, and it was overwhelmingly positive—94 percent—and UnMarketing was found to be the number one driver of mentions.

When I posted a blog sharing the story, some people commented that because I was already signed on as a spokesperson, this kind of thing was expected. I think it was even more awesome because they didn't have to do it, *because* I was already signed on. They took it that step further. The step was entirely unexpected, which is one of the reasons it had the effect that it did.

When you do awesome things, it makes people want to share the awesome.

It wouldn't matter how much they paid me; I would never have used my blog to promote ice cream. But I did, because of their awesome.

Well played, Duri and Magnum, well played indeed.

13

How to Apologize to a Woman

As a brand, their apology has been louder than the issue.

WHEN O.B. ULTRA TAMPONS returned to store shelves after being unavailable to customers for a year, the company decided to do something a little extra to apologize to their customers.

They created a video with a man (described online as "hunky") who sings a song saying sorry, especially for you. When you get to the site, it asks you to enter your name, and then for the next few minutes you are personally serenaded, complete with pictures of your name written across the sky, tattooed on the singer's arm, and written in rose petals.

Some sites online say that the video doesn't work for male names, but I beg to differ. Scott worked just fine.

The Toronto-based advertising agency Lowe Roche is behind the video. Loyal customers of the o.b. Ultra brand shared their disappointment online when the product was discontinued; one US site had a petition with 2,500 signatures and comments against Johnson

& Johnson, including a call for boycotts. In response, the company decided to bring back the popular product, plus a bonus song. At the end of the video, there is a $2 coupon, with the words "We owe you one."

What a great example of how to be awesome in PR. Johnson & Johnson didn't ignore their customers; in fact, they went above and beyond in their reply. They could have ignored the feedback and continued on with their long list of other products. Even if they had decided to bring back the product, they certainly didn't have to sing about it. Before seeing the apology video, I had no idea what they were apologizing for. As a brand, their apology has been louder than the issue. Not only have they answered and corrected their mistake, they bettered their brand image as a whole—and social media was the perfect tool to use.

The video is a brilliant use of technology. After all, you can't personalize a television commercial. The content is creative and fun to share. Who doesn't want to see her (or his!) name in rose petals? The appeal goes beyond the angry customers missing their product, beyond their static customer base, into their Third Circle (which is something we're going to talk about later when we look at Viral Marketing). You don't even have to be in their target market to think this video is great branding. Because content like this can be so easily spread online, it's the perfect space to use to improve brand image after a mistake. According to a study by Ogilvy and ChatThreads, social media is a top driver of brand perception impact, compared with the 20 channels they looked at and linked directly to brand perception.[1] That's compared with other channels such as television, radio, and other traditional marketing platforms.

This is a great example of a brand that faced serious backlash from a dedicated customer base and shows that not only can you make amends with them, but you can be awesome.

Even if you didn't know about the company or the product. Even if you never got upset or even noticed when it went missing from store shelves. Even if you're a dude like me who never thought you would want to. Check out the video from o.b. and see what an apology should look like: http://www.obtampons.ca/apology.

---

[1] http://corp.chatthreads.com/ChatThreads-Ogilvy-Social-Media-Impact-Study/.

14

How to Ship Out Your Reputation, and Then Return It

Absolutely, Positively Unacceptable.

THE PR DEPARTMENT REALLY EARNS its money when "it" really hits the fan and related negative discussions, videos, photos—whatever it is—take off online. People are very understanding of brands that show remorse, but it has to happen quickly. As you see over in the UnAwesome side, delaying that response by weeks, or even days, may as well be light-years in social media.

A great example of the value of a prompt PR recovery was FedEx's response after a video of one of their employees went viral back in December 2011. The video was a 10-second clip of one of their delivery drivers chucking a computer monitor over a fence, rather than ringing the bell at the gate and taking it to the front door. You can watch the video at http://bit.ly/UnDelivery.

The video could not have been shot more brilliantly. The camera angle showed both the driver walking up and the FedEx truck, complete with logo perfectly positioned in the background.[1] One guy, obviously dissatisfied with the service, shot and uploaded the video, and the geckalanche began. The UnAwesome spread, and millions of views poured in.

Faster than any brand I have ever seen, FedEx responded, and within a day or so, there was a blog posted to their corporate page, titled, "Absolutely, Positively Unacceptable."[2]

The post was thorough, showed remorse, and gave no excuses. Comments on the page were left open for anyone who wanted to contribute. An overwhelming percentage of these comments ended up being positive and supportive to the brand. They included a video of their senior vice president of US operations apologizing for the customer's experience and let everyone know publicly that they have resolved the issue with the customer and were disciplining the driver responsible. The apology was widely shared online. And although it did not catch up to the spread of the original video, it did hit the majority of their customer base.

As you can see by this, and the other examples we look at in this book that PR truly does stand for more than public relations; it stands for people react, people respond, and people reach out. People just want to be heard. As businesses, our reaction to people wanting to be heard is what separates the true PR professionals from the pretenders. PR can't function in a silo; they cannot be responsible only for what the company is saying but must also be responsible for what they are hearing. By focusing on immediacy, accountability, and personality, we truly can have a big impact on brands in real time. Let's put the public back into public relations.

---

[1]Seriously, it's like UPS set the whole thing up.
[2]http://bit.ly/FedExPR.

15

You Can't Ignore What You Hate

I hate FarmVille—mainly because I didn't invent it.

ONE OF THE MOST POPULAR EXCUSES I hear from people for not engaging on different online platforms is that they just don't like it, or get it. I hear things like, "Twitter is people saying what they had for lunch" or "Facebook is the place where all the people from high school I never liked hang out" or "How does any of this ever lead to a sale?" So I racked my brain for the perfect example for them—and you—of why you can't ignore what you hate, and I'm ready to talk about FarmVille.

If you've never heard of FarmVille, first, count your blessings; second, I want to be your friend on Facebook;[1] and third, let me explain. FarmVille is one of the most popular social games out there. Social gaming is any game played through social platforms, the most popular being Facebook. You log in with your Facebook account, you invite others to play with you, and you share game achievements on your wall.

---

[1] Seriously. Facebook.com/UnMarketing.

A company called Zynga created FarmVille and every other "Ville" game out there. On FarmVille, you can pretend to be a farmer, and it's just like being a farmer without all of the pesky farming parts. You plant virtual crops and tend to virtual cows, all with the click of a button. Sounds kind of lame, right? Tell that to the roughly quarter of a billion people who actively play Zynga's games on Facebook monthly.[2]

The game took in roughly $1 billion in 2011 alone, and it's a free game. They make money through in-app purchases, very small amounts at a time. A game like this is usually referred to as a freemium game, meaning the game is provided at no cost but a premium is charged for advanced features; these premiums result in a number of micro-transactions. Only 3 to 4 percent of players purchase anything, but with that many people playing, that's all you need.

I hate FarmVille—mainly because I didn't invent it. I've lost friends because of it. You can never look your buddy in the eye again after he writes "squeeeeeeee" on his Facebook wall because of a FarmVille accomplishment.

I may hate it, I may even loathe it, but I cannot ignore it. There are some fascinating aspects of community psychology at work in these types of games. Players are given in-game incentives for inviting new friends to the game. Achievements reward players for time on the game, and the game requires players to return daily to tend to their virtual farms.[3]

Here's the thing, no matter how much I may hate FarmVille, it is simply too successful to ignore. But the same thing applies to anything out there that you think is "not for you." At the very least, we need to be investigating these things if your demographic is there. For example, the demographic of a social gamer is not a 14-year-old boy. It's a 47-year-old woman. And 14 percent of social gamers play for more than four hours per day. How's that for blowing your mind and your preconceptions?!

So if that's your target demographic and you've been wondering where the heck they've been, they are just too busy tending their virtual farm to buy from you. Moooo . . .

---

[2]company.zynga.com.
[3]I have actually been asked to watch over people's farms while they were away on vacation. I'm waiting for the locust add-on package. I'd buy that.

16

The Only Good Use for QR Codes

He used QR codes to fight censorship and share his art.

I RANT A LOT about our online ADD and misuse of new, bright, and shiny technologies in business. One of my most popular videos online is all about QR codes and why they make the veins in my head pop out. It's pretty awesome; you should totally watch it: http://bit.ly/The ProblemWithQRCodes.

When Fredericton artist/photographer Jeff Crawford was asked to contribute some of his work to an exhibit at city hall, he faced a bit of a dilemma.

Figure 16.1   Jeff's New Art Piece Hanging in City Hall

The piece he wanted to include as part of the Fredericton Arts Alliance's Artists-in-Residence summer series included a nude woman. Not really a huge deal in art circles, but when you hang up art at city hall, you open yourself up to a whole lot of feedback.

Unfortunately, the picture was up for only half a day before city officials took it down after receiving a few complaints.

Jeff was asked for another piece of work. But he was pretty upset about the censorship, so he decided to do something about it. He sent city hall a new piece, framed and ready to be hung.

The framed image, which some of the people thought was the art, was a QR code[1]—in plain sight of passersby, some of whom were offended by his first picture (see Figure 16.1). When scanned, the code brings you to the original image on his website.

City hall was happy due to the lack of flesh. And Jeff was pleased because he didn't have to compromise his work. He used QR codes to fight censorship and share his art. I'm not really sure how you can use this in your business, but it does show that new technologies can do cool things when they work for you.

On the UnAwesome side of the book, we talk more about QR codes and why I don't think we should all be chasing after what's new and what's next. The thing is, like FarmVille, we can't ignore these things, either. The key is to check them out, see if they can bring us something that really helps our business, and if they do, use them appropriately. Jeff used QR codes as a tool to be awesome.

---

[1]http://bit.ly/QRAwesome.

17

Benefit of the Brand Doubt

Getting to know your customers is the key to creating brand security online.

So, AWESOME READERS, we've come this far together. We know that we should be listening to online conversations and looking for windows of awesome PR when things go wrong. We know that we can't shut off this listening in places we hate. We understand handing off the brand baton and how important it is to keep the awesome going throughout all parts of our business. And yet, we still find ourselves defending keeping our brand online and engaging with our market, or as I like to call it, talking with people.

As companies we get together once a year to discuss our brand definition, our brand statement, and other very fancy sounding ideas, when in reality, we don't define our brand at all. We can only try to influence thoughts about our brand. It's people outside of our company that define our brand for us. Our brand definition is in the hands not only of current customers but of anyone who has ever even heard of us. If someone has thought about your business, seen your advertising, walked past your office, visited your website, or seen your logo, he or she is part of shaping your brand perception.

When that person is asked, "What do you think about Brand A?" his or her answer is your brand statement. That answer varies both by individual and by day. Even the term *brand statement* is misleading. The word *statement* implies a fixed term, when in reality, it is a living, changing thing. And every action the company takes, or doesn't take, influences that potential statement.

Let's take a step back in the next few chapters and look at the bigger picture and awesome branding. How can online engagement shape overall perceptions and provide security for our company?

One of the biggest advantages to a brand being in social media is that it creates a personal connection that can lead to what I like to call benefit of the brand doubt or social security.

We're so trigger-happy when it comes to a poor brand experience. We are quick to tweet or post a rant on Facebook, acting before the brand has had time to fix an issue. Fear of customers' airing their negative experiences online is one of the main reasons brands worry about participating in social media in the first place. But really, the opposite is true. We are sharing negative experiences online anyway, whether the brand is there or not. Having your brand present on social media can actually protect its image against these negative messages.

Social media creates brand defenders,[1] those with a strong relationship with a brand who will take a stand for it publicly, when others are saying something negative. As a brand, you may not be able to be everywhere online or be able to reply to a customer as you would like to. How amazing it is to have loyal fans to do this for you! This happens most frequently on Facebook brand pages, where fans will come to the defense of a company if individuals are posting negative comments. Every brand defender you have online is another set of awesome ears, listening and ready to come to your side if something goes wrong online. These are also the eyes that catch potential customers, unhappy with your competitors and looking for recommendations online.

When you take the time to invest your brand's time and resources into creating relationships, your customers become less trigger-happy. They come to feel like they know you. This relationship creates trust;

---

[1] I'm picturing capes, leotards, and sponsorship patches all over.

then, when negative experiences happen, they give you a chance first—giving you the benefit of the brand doubt—privately sharing their concerns instead of publicly shaming you.

For example, when I used to do my work at Williams Café, I was able to send the owner, whom I knew personally, a private message if I ever had a problem at his restaurant. This gave him the opportunity to correct the issue, without the issue ever being made public. Think of the value to a brand in having customers feel secure enough and have a channel to share problems that could be used to potentially improve their businesses. I give this same benefit of the brand doubt to Disney, McDonald's, and Pepsi, all because I know someone personally in their organizations through Twitter.

Getting to know your customers is the key to creating brand security online. Not only does it lessen the impact of shared negative experiences and create a base of loyal defenders, it stops those negative stories from being voiced publicly in the first place. If earning the benefit of the brand doubt isn't a good enough reason to take your business online and make it awesome, then I don't know what is.

For updates and new stories about awesome branding, visit www.TheBookOfBusinessAwesome.com/Branding.

18

How to Spice Up an Old Brand

Marketing is more than sales; it can be about opening minds up to your brand.

IF YOU ARE A FELLOW MARKETER, please don't skip over this chapter because you think it's just another rehashing of how great the Old Spice Guy campaign is; there's more to it than that. For those of you who don't know the campaign, see http://on.mash.to/OldSpiceStats. In a nutshell, Old Spice took their popular Old Spice Guy character and had him respond to bloggers and Twitter questions from the shower, in almost real time. It was an amazing campaign and created a ton of buzz around the brand, not only because of how funny it was, but also because they were able to create and upload the video replies in a single day.

People in the industry argued back and forth about whether the campaign was successful. Some people wrongly thought sales didn't change. Others, when reading the sales numbers had increased, credited it to heavy couponing by Old Spice rather than the videos. But to me, sales numbers are only a small part of what the videos did, and the numbers and reasons behind them aren't even the point. Old Spice changed my viewpoint, and many others' viewpoints, about their brand. To my generation, Old Spice was what our fathers wore. I don't care if we are 80 years old; none of us wants to smell like our father.

Marketing is more than sales; it can be about opening minds to your brand. Changing brand perception is one of the hardest things to do in business. Once we, as consumers, decide what a product or company is all about, it is almost impossible to change our viewpoint. Social media is a perfect tool for brand recognition because it brings together everything: marketing, public relations, customer service, and branding.

One of the biggest problems with viral content is that the message outspreads the brand name. When the car ad with the Darth Vader kid goes viral, you remember the kid, but not the company. The video is hilarious, one of the most popular of the year, but if you ask people which car company was behind it, they are probably guessing. The Old Spice Guy is the Old Spice Guy. The name is right in the viral itself. You can't get any better than that in branding terms.

The campaign is the exact opposite of what people thought the brand was—old and stuffy. The campaign brought the product to present day, and did so in front of an entirely new audience and potential market. The value of that is more than a few months of sales numbers could ever show.

19

How Manya Made Vegas Awesome

A truly great voice from within your brand is worth more than a thousand crafted advertisements.

SOCIAL MEDIA PERSONALIZES BRANDS AND COMPANIES. The thing is, blurring the line between what is personal and what is business is always a challenge for people. Although we love a brand to have a face and a story, to be approachable and engaging, we also know that people are just that—people. And people make mistakes. When we spoke about PR earlier, we discussed that the message is now authentic and uncrafted. Well, authentic can be messy, and that can be a challenge in business.

On the other hand, when it works and a great personality comes through in a company, it is irreplaceable. Authenticity, by definition, cannot be faked. A truly great voice from within your brand is worth more than a thousand crafted advertisements.

When you run the show, you have the freedom to totally control your engagement. But when you work for someone else in a business setting, how social or personal should we get? Obviously in both situations, there is a line we don't want to cross, but when you work for someone else, how much of the awesomeness that is you should you bring to the social table?

Here is an example of someone I think does social from within a business the right way. We have since become great friends, but when we first met, it was because of business. A few years ago, I was looking to host my first tweet-up,[1] and I wanted to hold it somewhere in my favorite city: Las Vegas. After doing some searching on my own, I started reaching out to resorts, but all I got back was a lot of flack and a ton of resistance. I was looking for a section in a bar or a club that could seat 50 to 100 people, someplace to sit around and have drinks—all on an off-night for Vegas.[2] This was in the middle of the recession, and Vegas was one of the hardest hit cities during this terrible time for the economy. I couldn't understand why no one wanted my business.

The clubs wanted me to pay huge deposits and make guarantees, but I didn't understand why. I wasn't asking for the entire place to be shut down. I wanted to bring them some business, and 50 to 100 chances to impress people and maybe get some new fans, all on a usually quiet night for them. That's getting a whole lot of people in the door for the first time—one of the hardest things to do, especially in a town as full of options as Vegas.

As I'm sure you can imagine, I was getting frustrated. I told my friend Jess Berlin about the problems I was having. She was with social media for Cirque du Soleil at the time, and she directed me to a friend of hers, Manya Susoev. This is when everything changed for me—changed for the event, my experience in Vegas, and how I have continued to do business there.

Manya works for a company called Light Group, which owns a number of Las Vegas clubs. I called her and told my story, and we connected instantly. She understood what I was trying to do and actually gave a damn. She wanted my business. Instead of resisting and throwing up roadblocks, she was flattered I was talking to her and giving her the opportunity to help me out. She was empathetic to my

---

[1] A tweet-up is where Twitter geeks get together to actually talk face-to-face, instead of keyboard to keyboard.

[2] It wasn't exactly New Year's Eve or a *Hangover* reunion tour.

frustration and brought to the table a great understanding of how her industry works.

Manya was back in touch with me the next day with a bunch of options, which is all I had wanted and hoped for from the very beginning. We ended up using the top patio overlooking the strip at the awesome Diablo's, attached to the Monte Carlo. The event was amazing. I went from being treated like a small-time social media person to being treated like a VIP. I have been back to Vegas 26 times, and we've thrown all of our parties at Light Group establishments. At our last tweet-up there, also held on an off-night, the bar grossed about $6,000, a *substantial* improvement over what they would have typically made on such a night. That seems like good business to me.

If you want to measure the ROI of people, on social media, and on making business personal and engaging, look at what Manya did for the Light Group. I go to their clubs because of her.

There is the warning that goes along with that for companies. To me, Manya is the Light Group brand. I don't know anyone else there. If Manya goes, my loyalty goes with her, and whoever comes in next will have some big shoes to fill. So be careful about having one person be the only connector for your brand. We need to find the Manyas and value what they bring to the table.

In conclusion, although we don't define our brand internally, we certainly can influence it on both a marketwide scale and one to one. Our brand is what we do, not who we think we are. Brand statements, mission statements, and core company values are potentially useful internally in that they give a company a beacon to point its actions toward. But they are practically useless from the outside looking in. By realizing our brand definition is always changing, we won't sit back and talk about it only once a year, because we know people are talking about it every day. Thanks Manya, you deserve a raise.

20

Fractional Reaction

We need to manage the expectation of worth, of our social media audience size, before we brag about how big they are.

IF BRANDING IS THE DEFINITION of your company to your market, then viral is how that message gets out online. As we discussed when we were looking at branding, the same rule of control applies to viral marketing. You don't say what goes viral. You do not dictate what gets passed around. You can hope something will, you can enable tools to make it spread easily, but you cannot make something go viral. Viral marketing isn't a campaign, it's the goal of every campaign. When we hear the term *viral*, we usually think of cat videos,[1] but unless you're selling cat food, that really doesn't do anything for you. As you will see when we speak about Third Circle, people spread content because it's awesome.

In the first book, I spoke a lot about viral marketing, so it's not necessary to rehash too much about it here. What I do want us to

---

[1]Or the one with the talking dog . . . amazing: http://bit.ly/TalkingDogVid.

talk about is one of the biggest misconceptions about viral when it comes to the numbers. With the explosion of social media, as we count and focus on followers and likes, we can get a falsely inflated sense of audience size. One thousand followers, or fans, is not the same as a thousand newsletter subscribers or a thousand-person customer list. Social media is the definition of what I call fractional reaction.

Fractional reaction is a way of understanding reach in social media. For example, if you have 1,000 followers, of those 1,000, 10 percent will be online at any given time. Of those, 10 percent will see your tweet and 10 percent of that 10 percent will click on the link in the tweet. So 1,000 followers equaled one click. When I tweet a picture to more than 100,000 followers, on average, it will get about 1,000 views. Tweets and Facebook statuses all have short shelf lives because of how quickly new content is put up by everyone else.

Even if you had a million followers and wanted them to buy something on your website, the fraction ends up being pretty small. Of the million, 100,000 are online, 10,000 will see the tweet, 1,000 will click the link, and 30 will click to order, with only 20 completing the purchase. All these numbers change with an engaged audience, because the original post will end up ranking higher on Facebook and being shared more across all platforms. But the concept is still really important, because we need to manage the expectation of worth, of our social media audience size, before we brag about how big they are.

For updates and new stories about viral, visit www.TheBookOf BusinessAwesome.com/Viral.

21

Third Circle

This is what viral is all about. It's not about numbers; it's about reach.

WHETHER IT'S A VIDEO, a blog post, or even a picture, everyone wants his or her content to go viral. And there are almost as many people telling you how to make your stuff "go viral" as there are horrible videos on YouTube with 20 views.[1]

Let's think about our social space and how information and ideas are shared. We start by putting ourselves in the center (Figure 21.1).

Figure 21.1 You

Closest around us is our First Circle, where we find current friends of us personally and of our brand (Figure 21.2). These are our strongest connections, our solid clients and rabid fans. These are the people who will always share your content, sometimes without even looking at it. They know if you liked it, they will. No matter what.

---

[1] Twelve of which are the creator clicking refresh.

Figure 21.2   First Circle

Beyond them is your Second Circle (Figure 21.3). Here the connections to you are weaker. These are the friends of your First Circle—the ones they reach out to. These people always have access to your content through your loyal fans; they will probably give your content a look, but they can't be counted on to always share. It is really easy to lose this circle's attention and trust with bad content. A few disappointing clicks, and they won't be coming back easily.

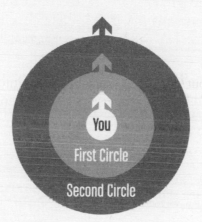

Figure 21.3   Second Circle

The trick is getting this Second Circle to pass content along to their circles, thereby creating the Third Circle (Figure 21.4).[2] This is the group you need to be thinking about when you're creating content. If you can reach the Third Circle, you have now reached people who, for the most part, have no connection to you personally or to your

---

[2]This gets dangerously close to *Lord of the Rings* territory here. I apologize, my precious.

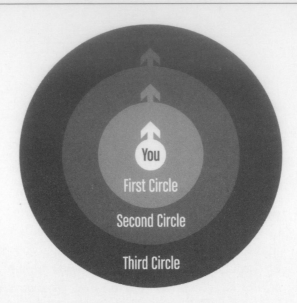

Figure 21.4   Third Circle

brand. So, without any personal relationship to the content, they are spreading the information based solely on quality. People share content online because it's awesome, not because it's yours.

This is why commercials don't go viral. Brand fans share the commercial because they love the brand, but once their Second Circle sees it, the connection is lost and it stops being shared. I've seen brands try to force viral, where to enter a contest you have to share some of their content. This rarely gets past the First Circle. Sharing stuff online not because it's good but because you must to get something out of it can really hurt the social reputation of the people sharing it. The same goes for all the "vote for me" contests, where we exhaust our social reach by cyber-begging for votes for inane contests. I don't see the value in risking a hard-earned social reputation to be named one of the top 12,000 mom bloggers in the Western Hemisphere. The site running the contest gains traffic, but you lose social standing with friends and followers. Sharing conditionally is not the answer to making something truly go viral; it has to be organic.

To break through to the next circle, your content needs viral velocity—that is, enough energy and enough awesome to make people *need* to share it with their circles, independent of their connections to you. The content needs to stand alone and stand out.

This is what viral is all about. It's not about numbers; it's about reach. If I create a ridiculous video of a cat meowing the "Thong

Song" (that's in your head now, you're welcome) and send it out to my 100,000 followers and it gets 1,000 views, that is not viral. Now if someone else made it and sent it to 20 people and it ended up with 1,000 views, that is viral. It spread outside the original circles.

You can count on that second video to continue getting views as time passes, while mine dies out. This is where you truly can remedy the fractional reaction issue. You may have a small following yourself, but the viral nature of the content will mean that the fractional reaction will be exponentially higher, because more than one person will be sharing it with their First Circle.

You can also reach the Third Circle through slow and steady quality content. Everyone wants the one big hit, but really a career of high-quality content, shared with continuity, is the real prize online. To be able to gain the Second Circle's trust with solid content over time, growing your First Circle and continuing to get your content into new hands, is the goal. One-hit wonders may get a large amount of fleeting views, but a strong base of quality material enables the body of your content to reach a large audience over time.

A good personal example of Third Circle for me is Boyce Avenue. One of my friends on Facebook posted Boyce Avenue's YouTube video of them covering the Tracy Chapman song "Fast Car." And so I clicked on it. It was an awesome cover, and I decided to not only share it with others online but also clicked on the iTunes link and bought the album. A friend of mine in the UK, Elysia Brooker, saw me share it, and knowing my absolutely incredible taste in music, decided to watch it as well. She loved the song, listened to a few others, and went to their website, where she learned that they were going to be in the UK on tour—and then bought tickets to the show.

The band themselves could never have gotten me to listen to a song directly. There are so many musicians and videos online, it's easy to get lost in the crowd. It was my First Circle trust with the friend who shared it that made me willing to give them a try. Here is the link to the song if you want to watch it yourself. Hope you enjoy it as much as I did http://bit.ly/BoyceAvenueFastCar.

22

Reflecting on Awesome

All social media–driven and 100 percent awesome; it doesn't get much better than that.

FOR ME, ONE OF MY BEST EXAMPLES of creating content that reached the Third Circle is ReflectionsOfMotherhood.com, a campaign we put together for Alison Kramer, owner of Nummies Bras. We were looking for a way to inspire moms, while also getting in front of them. Our goal was to create something for moms that they would enjoy without feeling like they were watching a commercial.

The whole project was created and driven through social media. Starting with a blog post, where Alison asked moms what advice they would go back and give themselves before having their first child. The post and answers were put together and we then invited moms online to come out to a photo shoot for the project.

The result was a series of photos, set to music, of moms holding up signs with the advice that spoke most to them.

As you can see on the website, the results are pretty awesome. Advice like "Sleep now" and "Google doesn't have children" ended up being especially popular. The video is a great case study for using social media in business. Most of the moms in the video came out because of the tweet looking for participants, and the ideas started with a blog post asking moms what they would tell themselves looking back. Even the brilliant photographer Sara Collaton was found on Twitter.

It has received more than half a million views, all because it reached that Third Circle, and here are some of the reasons why.

1. **Now is not the time to be modest; the idea was awesome.** We came up with a great idea and knew right away people would love it. People ask us all the time if we knew it would be as popular as it ended up being, and the truth is, we loved it so much we knew other people would, too. If you're not excited about your idea, why would anyone else be?

2. **It is not a commercial.** You don't need to buy anything, like anything, or sign up for anything to watch and enjoy "Reflections." This was very important to Alison and really the only way you know it was from her company is because of the picture at the end of her saying thank you. And she had to be convinced to even do that.

3. **YouTube doesn't make anything go viral, but it does help something already taking off to continue going.** By not having to worry about bandwidth or how many people are watching something at one time (things you would have to worry about if you had it on your own server), the video was free to be seen by as many people as wanted.

4. **No restrictions were put on sharing it.** Settings were adjusted on purpose to allow the video to be embedded on anybody's site. So they could share in the viral. A lot of brands lock down this function, wanting to own all the views, but that is a huge mistake. This video was embedded on practically every major parenting website in the world. Just remember, this is why you should identify your company somewhere inside the video.

5. **It's mobile-friendly.** Another big reason to use YouTube is that it can play on all smartphones. One problem you can run into is with music copyright, for example; if you use someone else's song, there may be restrictions, and one of the common ones is that it won't play on a mobile device. We were lucky that the band

InAshton[1] not only let us use their song but recorded a customized version for us.

6. **The visuals are awesome.** The photos were strong, because we hired Sara Collaton,[2] a professional photographer, to take the photos. She captured the emotion in everyone's faces.

7. **We had a broad topic.** Although Alison's target market for the most part is new moms, this video was broad enough in topic that many moms wanted to share it. Grandmothers, mothers, daughters, fathers, and sons even wanted to pass it along. This is a huge part of reaching the Third Circle. The topic of the video didn't deter people from sharing it. You didn't have to be nursing or even be a woman to enjoy it.

"Reflections" is continually reaching a new audience. Every day, Nummies receives e-mails from parents who are touched by the images and message of the video, which is both strong and evergreen (see Figure 22.1). All social media-driven and 100 percent awesome, it doesn't get much better than that. If you haven't seen the video, or just want to watch it again, you can check it out at www. ReflectionsofMotherhood.com. Just be warned you might want to grab a Kleenex, it's been known to make a mom or two, and even a dad, cry.

Figure 22.1   Last Scene of Reflections of Motherhood

Source: Sara Collaton. Used with permission.

[1]http://inashton.com/.
[2]http://www.saracollaton.com/.

23

Part Man, Part Machine, All Crowdfunded

The power of an online community with a shared interest is immeasurable.

As HUMANS, we want to connect and we want to belong. The nature of how and why we share content online makes it a perfect space for charity marketing and fund-raising, which is usually emotive, with strong images and easily relatable. Causes such as ending child hunger, ending homelessness, and fighting cancer have all found a strong online voice in social media. Taking your cause online can raise awareness and dollars.

When a cause means something to a friend, it means something to us. That is a great advantage of building a personal network of people. We give a damn about one another and our causes. Every tweetathon I have helped with, and every cause I have donated to online, was a direct result of a friend of mine bringing the need to my attention.

One of my favorite examples of a site encouraging and facilitating online giving is Kiva.com. Founded in 2005, Kiva is an amazing example of a worldwide network that uses crowdsourcing to fund projects. You can go to the site and make a donation of as little as $25 toward a variety of projects, including housing developments, agriculture projects, or anything from an individual starting a small business to a community funding a large effort. The borrowers meet with Kiva partners and receive loans from local microfinance institutions, which the site calls Field Partners. The Partners assess what is needed and whether it will work on the site, and then the loans are posted to Kiva.com with descriptions. One hundred percent of every donated dollar goes to the lenders, and when the loan is paid off, it appears as a credit in your Kiva account. You can then choose to reloan the money or use it for another purpose.

At the time of this writing, the site says that 4,854 new lenders have joined, almost 40,000 loans were given, more than 1,000 Kiva cards (which are used to give someone money to use for loans on the site) were purchased, and $3,437,625 was loaned, funding more than 7,000 entrepreneurs. Those are some powerful numbers.

Using online communities is not only for charities. You can also use crowdsourcing or crowdfunding to get other kinds of projects off the ground. One of the most well-known sites in the arts community is Kickstarter.com. Their tagline is "A new way to fund and follow creativity."

You can go to the site and browse all sorts of projects, from bands trying to record albums, artists trying to open art exhibits, to those wanting to produce feature-length movies. The incentive to donate is driven by reward levels. One of the projects I funded was Paco the Judo Popcorn, a cartoon about a piece of corn skilled in martial arts.[1] They had different incentives in place, depending on your donation amount. If you gave a small amount, you received some stickers; those who donated a top amount received credit at the end of the show as an executive producer. I chose to make a donation of $100, solely to get a T-shirt of this feisty piece of popcorn, along with some other things.

The great thing about setting donation levels with incentives is that it inspires people to donate more than originally intended. I've

---

[1] Tell me you wouldn't want to be a part of that, too.

funded everything from this cartoon, to a photography exhibit in Kentucky, to an app for the iPad, to an art house in Detroit.

People love to feel part of something, especially when there is an exclusive reward involved. In February of 2012, Kickstarter reached an incredible milestone and had not one, but two projects reach goals of one million dollars, all within 24 hours. At the end of the day, though, the project needs to be compelling so that it stands out from the many options out there to give money to—on this site and others. And since you usually don't receive a tax deduction with the donation, the project has to be that much more awesome.

My awesome crowdsourcing favorites are some fellows in Detroit who decided that they needed to erect a statue of a well-known local hero but were turned down for funding due to economic restraints. This wasn't going to be a statue of the mayor, an industry leader, or even Eminem. This was to be a statue of Robocop, and that is awesome. They turned to Kickstarter.com to find funding for the creation of the statue, and people from around the world donated. You can follow along and see all the donations at www.detroitneedsrobocop.com.

If you're sitting there reading this and getting ready to fund your project online, it's important to note when you set your fund-raising goal, you don't receive any of the donations unless this goal number is met or exceeded. In regard to Robocop, the goal was met and exceeded quickly and ended up raising $67,000, through donations from 2,700 people. Many, many people "bought that for a dollar."[2]

The power of an online community with a shared interest is immeasurable. Our ability to all come together, each giving a little, adds up to a whole greater than the sum of its parts. The problem with showing you these successful case studies is that people start talking about social return on investment, or SROI. Trying to equate talking with revenue can become really dangerous. Revenue should not be seen as a goal but rather as the result of being a great social company.

---

[2] This line means more if you've seen the movie. If you haven't seen the movie, I feel sorry for you. Stay away from the sequels!

24

The Social Media ROI Conversation

If we don't value conversation, we will never see why we need to use social media.

Scene 1. The boardroom conversation with your boss, aka ROI Guy.

You: I'd like to spend some time replying to customers on social media.

ROI Guy: What the heck is social media?

You: Oy.

ROI Guy: Give it to me in English.

You: Our customers are talking about our products online and asking questions. I'd just like to be able to answer them. There's almost a billion people on Facebook alone.

ROI Guy: You mean spend your work time on BookFace and Tweezer? That's crazy talk, we run a real business here. (*Throws up arms.*)

You: People talking about our products is our business. I want us to be a part of the conversation before our competitors are.

ROI Guy: I told you; I don't speak Spanish. What you are saying does not make sense. What is the ROI of this social media?

You: Asking the return on investment on social media is like asking what the ROI of our phone is.

ROI Guy: Listen, fancy pants, in the real world we have to justify everything we spend money on. ROI is for grown-ups and serious businesspeople. (*Throws arms up.*)

You: Oh really, what's the ROI of the 5,000 golf balls you got last week with our logo?

ROI Guy: Don't bring the golf balls into this; they look so cool with our little logo on them flying through the air. It's priceless.

You: Or what's the ROI of this new boardroom table here that you just paid $25,000 for?

ROI Guy: Are you mental? That's just crazy talk. Look how delicious this table looks. It shows clients that we're sophisticated and professional.

You: I think answering their questions on social media looks pretty sophisticated and professional.

ROI Guy: This is just an excuse so you can play FarmVille at work. Isn't it?

You: Good lord . . . I understand we have to justify what we do with our time. I just don't think social media should be held to a higher standard than everything else. How much was our last Yellow Pages ad?

(*continued*)

(*continued*)

ROI Guy: $15,000. But, they threw in some golf balls with their logo on them.

You: When a customer phones, what do we do?

ROI Guy: We answer the phone.

You: When they e-mail, what do we do?

ROI Guy: We reply.

You: And when they tweet, what should we do?

ROI Guy: No idea.

You: Ugh . . . If we don't value conversation, we will never see why we need to use social media. Can I at least use LinkedIn for a bit?

ROI Guy: Why?

You: To find a new job.

ROI Guy: Touché.

To see this live in action, check out the blockbuster animated flick. I'm open to offers from DreamWorks. http://bit.ly/ROIConversation.

25

Before Social ROI

Remember that business is personal.

"WHAT'S THE ROI OF SOCIAL MEDIA?" That question gives me ulcers when asked it. Easy now, old-school business folk; I don't have a problem questioning the value or return on something that takes potentially both time and money from your business. Any smart businessperson would do that.

My problem is how we hold social media to a higher level of judgment than most things in business.

So, at no charge, I will Skype into any of your companies and explain exactly what the ROI of social media is—if you first can tell me what the ROI is of the following 11 common business practices:

1. **Meetings.** Especially meetings about how social media is a waste of time. Weekly meetings . . . with 10 people in attendance.
2. **CC'ing everybody on every e-mail.** I figure in the time it takes to read every "official" corporate e-mail, you could've built a Twitter

empire, ruled Facebook, and had time to play some Angry Birds (on Google+).

3. **Meetings.**
4. **Those 2,000 mugs with your logo.** I know that when I need a lawyer, I search my coffee mug shelf. I know, I know, you bought them in December so you could spend your budget in order to get it again next year, but still.
5. **Overpaid conference keynote speakers.** No, wait. Scratch that. Nothing to see here. Move along.[1]
6. **Meetings.**
7. **Making your employees commute.** Your business is mostly done over the computer or on the phone. Why do they have to sit at a desk again? Face time FTW!
8. **Leather boardroom blotters.** Ask the administrative assistant who is on year 5 of a wage freeze how impressed he or she is that you just spent $2,000 on leather squares.
9. **Meetings.**
10. **Your Yellow Pages ad, direct-mail pieces, and trade show booth.** If you know the exact ROI on these three, awesome; you're ahead of the game. Most, however, have no clue.
11. **Fax machines and toner.** Seriously. I had a vendor say I couldn't e-mail a scanned version of a contract to them because they needed me to "fax the original." You know the actual piece of paper doesn't travel through the phone line, right? Right??

We know that to be successful in business, we have to:

- Answer questions about our product or service.
- Educate consumers.
- Offer post-purchase follow-up.
- Market research.
- Discuss industry best practices.

Read those five things to a social media naysayer and ask if that person agrees that they are smart for businesses—because that's a checklist for what social media is used for. Just sayin'.

---

[1]Check out my speaking site www.ScottStratten.com.

Remember that business is personal. Businesspeople don't join social media because "people talk about what they had for lunch or a movie they're going to see." But that's the whole point. It's not called epic fact media or business media. It's social. If you stopped referring to people as "leads" all the time, you may realize that the days when you were to leave "personal matters at the door" and change into business mode no longer exist.

It is simply not good business to judge social media to a higher set of standards than you would answering your phones or replying to e-mails. Ignoring the conversation customers are having about your brand every day is bad business. Paying attention to your market and potential customers is good business. It's as basic as that. Although it is true that the online conversation can sometimes be casual and more personal than a formal letter, why should the standards of deciding value be different than those of a networking event or company golf trip? Business is personal, and great businesses show awesome personality, online and offline.

26

Connect Outside Your
Field of Vision

The meeting of the minds is an extremely beneficial thing.

IF YOU'VE BEEN IN BUSINESS for any reasonable amount of time, you understand the value of networking. You get it.

One of the things that social media does is increase our ability to network outside our field of vision. To network past what we can see. Networking is usually confined to chamber of commerce and local business events or to annual conferences. I don't know about you, but I learn a heck of a lot when I'm at these events and talking with my peers, especially when these conversations are with peers outside my geographic region. We allow these connections to be so much more honest—truer—because these peers are not usually direct competitors. When you have a local-based business, you should be looking at networking opportunities outside your field of vision—and that's exactly what social media can give you the opportunity to do.

Let's say you have decided that social media isn't for you. You've decided it isn't the best place to have conversations with your customers. Maybe you are in business in an area where no one is using Twitter or Facebook (maybe a town of six people, five of whom don't have a computer). Now, I'm not sure where this mythical place is, or why you have chosen to be in business there, but nonetheless, you have resigned yourself to saying, "Ya know what, this social media thing is not for me." You've decided your customers aren't there and it's too time and labor intensive.

The thing is, even if you're right, your peers are there. There are other people who do what you do, who share your passions and work within your field online right now. These are the people who you can't really talk to locally, because they may be your competition. And here they are—online, outside of your area, and just waiting for someone to talk to. Maybe it's real estate or dentistry. Whatever the business may be, you don't want to share your trade secrets with another local business who may use them. But online, you are in Toronto and the other person is in Dallas, so there is no business threat. These are the people you need to be talking to, but because they're outside your field of vision, you usually don't.

Even if you aren't using it already, go to social media sites and search for people in your industry. Look for people in your field, outside your field of vision and competitive circle. Learn from them; connect with them. The meeting of the minds is an extremely beneficial thing. Learn from one another's mistakes, learn from one another's best practices, and be truly honest about what we all do—because we don't have to be in the same room to network anymore.

27

Peripheral Referrals

People in social media aren't leads; they are people. They are connections.

WE ALL KNOW THAT REFERRALS are the number one way to grow our businesses. The most effective way, the most desired way, and the cheapest way to gain new business is to have happy current customers who let others know how awesome you are.

In a classic business model, one of the things that never happens is referral from noncustomers, those who have yet to use your product or service. I mean, how could they, right? Without social media, if you asked me about finding a pool cleaner and I didn't own a pool, what could I say? Google it?

Social media has changed this by opening up the avenue I call social referrals—referrals from people who have not yet used your product or service but who have gotten to know, like, and trust you online.

Now, when someone asks me if I know a pool cleaner, even if I don't have a pool, I go to my online community. Because social media is all about conversation, we connect with people about many things.

So I may know someone online because we've spoken about parenting, or travel or our love of how many people Rob Base and DJ E-Z Rock say it takes to make things go right,[1] but it turns out they are also a pool cleaner. Now I know someone in the industry online even though I've never needed their services. I can also tweet out to my followers for recommendations. Social media has allowed me to get to know people in countless industries whose services and products I have yet to use myself—but to whom I would still give a social referral.

The more people you know, and more important, the more people who know you (even before they have been your customer), the greater your social network. The old idea of focusing on talking only to leads, or even referring to people as leads, is dying. People in social media aren't leads; they are people. They are connections. And when these connections grow, others get to know, like, and trust us, even without ever having used our products or services.

Social referrals are so easy to give. They aren't highly committal, like other kinds of referrals. Today, people are usually hesitant to give referrals, especially publicly. You need to lend your name, credibility, and trust with a referral. But a social referral isn't like that. You can say, "I've never used this company before, but I know them online and Chris over there seems like a great real estate agent or a great guy. Why don't you read their stuff and get to know them first." You aren't on the hook for the referral, but you were able to help an online friend who was looking for a connection by suggesting someone. Win, win, win.

The larger and more engaged your social network is, the better your referral network is. This works both ways. Not only do we gain referrals and grow our own business, but we can also access the network when we are the customer looking for products or services. When I need to find someone to work with in business, I don't go to the Yellow Pages and I don't Google the term; I tweet about it. I ask my network for trusted referrals. What is the value to you in building a community where you can ask advice of people you trust—both personally and professionally? What is the value in not wasting your time and money on a product or service because you asked first and were given recommendations online? I think trusted referrals alone are worth all the time and energy spent engaging online.

---

[1] The answer is two.

28

7 Dollars and an iROI, Lessons in Social Return on Investment

Building up your social network has countless advantages, not the least of which is that there is a club of people around the world who give a damn about you.

PEOPLE LIKE TO DO BUSINESS with people they know, like, and trust. This is really the basis of any talk about ROI from social media. This success is highly dependent on the individuals executing the engagement; their techniques are more important than the tools they are using. This is why you can't make it as simple as saying a platform works or doesn't, because it is so important who is there representing your brand. You can't blame the hammer for not working when it is the carpenter who's all thumbs. The people make the difference.

One great example of this for me is my introduction to and future work with Tungle.me. As I was planning the UnBook Tour last year, a friend of mine, DJ Waldow, sent me a phone conference invite through Tungle.me. I'd never heard of the service before and assumed it was just another online service that I'd need to sign up for. I checked out the site anyway and quickly realized that the interface was actually kind of cool. The best part was, I didn't have to sign up to try it; I could just use it. I was happy about it, so I tweeted about it.

The account @TungleRocks tweeted me right back with a thank you. I was impressed, and we chatted for a bit. To make a long story short, by the following week, I was on the phone with Richard Zeidel and Jonathan Levitt, key executives at Tungle, talking about Tungle and their plans for the business. I gave them my feedback, and we kept in touch.

Fast-forward a month. We were discussing BlogWorld, which I was keynoting, and Tungle decided to sponsor my party at the event. Going back and forth about sponsorship was new to me, and I had no idea how much to ask for. I kept picturing myself asking for $7. Thankfully, the crew at Tungle were amazing and a pleasure to work with—as awesome throughout as their product was and as they had been since that first tweet. They ultimately ended up sponsoring not only the party but also all the lead-up tour stops to the event. I even ended up on their board of advisors, giving me equity in the company. All of this was because of the relationship one tweet started.

Back to my original point: the tweet didn't create the ROI; it was the relationship that was formed afterward and the quality of the product beforehand. ROI is rarely created directly on the social media platform, but it is that platform that leads to the ROI. Twitter was the tool that brought us together, but it wasn't the reason for success—that was all about Tungle and their awesomeness.

Sometimes ROI can be measured only in degrees of awesome, and at other times it can be measured in iPads, which brings me to my second example. Building up your social network has countless advantages, not the least of which is that there is a club of people around the world who give a damn about you. This was proved to me when I flew to Texas to keynote an event[1] and left my iPad in the seat pocket on the plane.

This was, unfortunately, my second time leaving my iPad somewhere. When I realized it was gone, I was ready to write it off as my regular bimonthly iPad purchase, but things went differently this time.

---

[1] www.SummerBrandCamp.com.

I decided to send out a distress tweet, which, by the way, is one of the only times I will ever write in all caps. I tweeted that I left my iPad on an American Airlines flight to Texas. Then, after following the usual communication channels, phoning the airline and airport, and filing a report, I went to bed, knowing that I might never see my best friend, nay, my soul mate, ever again.

I awoke in the morning to multiple phone messages and e-mails letting me know that my iPad had been found! I was incredibly surprised, especially because the plane I had left it on had already left for Mexico by the time I realized what had happened. I figured it had long ago been traded for an all-inclusive vacation.

So, how was my iPad saved? My distress tweet had been seen overnight by Ruth, a follower of mine who runs the Twitter account @SeriouslySofas. (Serendipitously, she had recently joined Twitter after hearing me speak in England.) Ruth happened to be good friends with an executive for American Airlines. Ruth e-mailed Marie K. Jary, American Airlines director of regional sales for the Midwest, in the middle of the night, asking her for help hunting down my lost iPad. After finding it and arranging to get it to me, the manager of the regional American Eagle Airline showed up 10 minutes before my keynote was to start and handed me my iPad. I took it on stage and said proudly, "You want social media ROI? Here's your ROI!" And held the iPad up in the sky.

One of the best things about social media is how it can create a true community. Having a virtual network of people helping one another is enough ROI for me. And getting my iPad back didn't hurt either.

The tweet alone wasn't what brought my iPad back to me; it was how people reacted to it, how they took the conversation and ran with it. Getting to know and care about one another is the real investment, and the return can really be endless.

29

30 Tips for Speakers

You are up on that stage for a reason.

WHEN WE TALK ABOUT THE ROI of social media, the investment part is usually seen as time spent online. However, one of the coolest things about building a platform online is how we can end up growing an offline community around it as well. I have met more caring, intelligent, funny people through Twitter than through any other platform before, online or offline. Creating these relationships and a platform online has changed my business and led to my sole business function now being speaking to audiences around the world.

Speaking at events is a great way to generate potential business and position yourself as an expert in your field. However, it can hurt you more than it helps if not done properly. My main source of revenue now, outside of the 86 cents I made on your buying this copy of the book, is speaking. I have to bring value to any event I'm a part of. Problems usually occur when somebody speaks for free and needs to make money by selling from the stage. Those talks end up being a commercial, simply not valuing the audience's time or providing any real content.

If you're already a speaker, or thinking of getting into it, I have put together a collection of 30 tips that may help things go more smoothly for you on stage.

1. **Be you.** When you try to be someone else on stage, it makes you even more nervous. I dress like me, I talk like me, and I say what I think. I tell stories. That may not be your style. People will try to knock that out of you. Just in the past two days, one person said I should have better "hygiene" and wear a tie (I wear a black shirt and have facial hair). Another person said I was "over the top" with how I speak. What you don't hear is the silent majority who like you being you and who are relieved that it isn't another stuffed-up suit and tie on stage; and for some of us, "over the top" means really freaking passionate about what we say. I ain't changing that for anybody. And neither should you.

2. **But, remember, it's not about you.** Every time you take the stage in front of an audience, you need to be thinking about them. What are they looking for? Where are they in terms of how much they know and understand about your topic? I give a very different talk to a crowd who throws up no hands when I ask, "Who has a Twitter account?" than to a social media club. To make it great for every audience, you need to make it about your audience.

3. **Don't be a "speaker." Be an expert who speaks.** Speakers are a "nice to have," but experts are a necessity. There is a high demand for people who can both provide content and deliver it effectively from the stage. Some can do one of the two, most don't do either, and a select few do both. Aim to be great.

4. **Have passion for what you're saying.** If you don't, your audience won't, either. You are up on that stage for a reason.

5. **Think about what new ideas or skills your audience will have when they leave your session.** If the only answer you have for this question is, "They'll know more about me!" you need to start over. "Know your audience. There is a big difference between talking to 5th graders and mid-level corporate executives. The more that you know and tailor, the better the speech will be."[1]

---

[1] From David Siteman Garland, http://www.therisetothetop.com.

6. **Ask for a cell number of the conference organizer if you have to travel to speak there and text them when you get in safely.** A less stressed meeting planner/client means a happier one, too. This goes double if you're the opening keynote the next day.

7. **Make your organizers feel special.** Record a video shout out[2] to the conference's potential attendees and let them get to know you. It can be only a minute or two long—just enough to allow the client to use the clip on its blog/site to help generate buzz for the event.

8. **Change your presentation every time you give it.** Update stats; bring new examples. Own the content; don't repeat it. This is especially true in a field like social media, where what "we know" is changing so quickly. You really need to be on top of things. Setting up a Google Alert on different topics will ensure you know about current related news stories and events. If you've given a certain presentation numerous times and feel it's routine, either change it up or trash it. It may be the 20th time you've told a story, but it's the first time that audience has heard it.

9. **Do some pre-talk connecting.** If the conference has a #hashtag on Twitter, start finding people who are going to be there by searching with it. Talk to them, build relationships, and then track them down at the event to say hi. It'll be like you already know them, because you do.

10. **Do some pre-talk research.** Watch Twitter for mentions of your talk and let people know you appreciate them spreading your word. Post helpful tips that have to do with your content by using the same hashtag for the conference. It's a great way to connect with your audience and also find out what kind of things they are looking for in your talk.

11. **Respect your audience's time**. Right before you go on, clarify by what time they need you to wrap up your talk. If you were told an hour originally, and the previous speaker runs over his or her time, it's up to you to see if they need you to compress your talk or go the full hour. Nothing is more stressful for a conference than one that is running late.

---

[2]http://bit.ly/UnShoutOut.

12. **Arrive early and end your presentation early**. It is always great to leave time for questions and/or feedback from the audience. You don't want to have to rush off stage. Getting to know the audience beforehand and talking to them afterward to answer questions is a forgotten thing that brings the highest value.

13. **The power is not the point.** Slides are there as navigation points, not to be the content. If everything you say is on your slides, you've rendered yourself useless. Speak; don't read. You should also be prepared to present without slides in case something goes wrong. And then do it on purpose. Speakers are at their best during Q&A because they're not handcuffed to a slide. Think about that.

14. **Don't use video/Flash/audio in your slides**. Your slides should be able to play on a Commodore 64. Don't be "that guy" with custom fonts and dancing babies on the screen unless you're bringing your own laptop. If you do insist on using your own laptop, then arrive early enough to allow time for it to be set up properly. And for the love of the late Steve Jobs, bring a dongle, MacFanBoy.

15. **Respect the A/V and conference crew**. If you walk in front of the audio speakers or don't come early for the sound check, don't throw the look of death at the A/V people when your mic doesn't work right away. Those A/V people have seen 1,324 speakers this year already; they don't need Mr. Death Stare throwing them under the bus to the audience when it wasn't their fault in the first place. My goal is to make the A/V crew enjoy my talk. If you can please them, you can please anybody in that room. Oh, and if they don't like you, they can make you sound less pristine.

16. **Don't sell from the stage**. If you start every point with "In my book . . . ," you're doing a commercial, not a seminar. The best way to sell is to teach. I'm not saying ignore that you have a book, just simmer down a bit; we heard you the first five times.

17. **Follow cell phone best practices.** No matter how many times you remind people, someone's cell phone will go off during your talk. Get over it. Also, be sure your own cell phone is off before speaking.

18. **Be more interesting than Angry Birds**. You're not their parent. Don't tell them to put phones away; just ask as a courtesy to put the ringer on silent. I don't understand speakers who tell audiences they can't text or tweet during a talk. Make your content so good

that people feel they *have to* tell others right away but great enough that they don't want to miss a word.

19. **Use a handheld clicker for slides instead of using the laptop.** And when the audience doesn't see the hand clicker, you look like Obi-Wan Kenobi when the slide progresses on its own. I use Kensington 33374 Wireless Presenter with Laser Pointer.

20. **Don't focus on mistakes.** Don't apologize to the audience about something they wouldn't know was wrong. Saying "I was supposed to have a video here" doesn't help. Keep going.

21. **Think about how you begin.** "When the introducer says, 'Please give a warm welcome to Jim Smith,' don't start your talk with 'Hi, I'm Jim Smith.' And don't thank them for the warm welcome or start listing all the organizers you want to thank. You can weave that into the talk. Start with a powerful statement, an intriguing question, or other compelling beginning that will rivet their attention."[3]

22. **Try being a storyteller.** "Tell great stories (your own, not someone else's), and be funny. Don't tell jokes, but use humor."[4]

23. **Leave time for Q&A.** "Taking questions after your talk is a great way to close off a session. When a participant asks a question, remember to repeat the question for the audience. There's a chance that others, especially those at the back, didn't hear it."[5]

24. **Create usable feedback pages.** To get the most out of your feedback sheets, create two checkboxes at the bottom. One that says "I would like to be subscribed to your newsletter that provides [insert awesome benefit]" and the other that says "I know of a group/association that would benefit from your talk; drop me a line." Extend the contact past the session.

25. **Handle feedback wisely.** If you use feedback sheets, there will always be somebody who didn't like you. If it's in the majority, you need to consider what's said. If it's in the minority, ignore it.

26. **Value your time.** Speaking for free is a great lead generator and a quick way to go broke. Get value one way or another because you give it. Get conference passes for others, barter for product or

---

[3]From Randy Gage, http://www.randygage.com/blog/.
[4]From Ava Diamond, http://www.feistywomenrock.com/.
[5]From Sherine Clarke.

services, or at least negotiate for a wheel of cheese. Think about your stress points, too. If taking a taxi from an airport in a city you don't know is hard for you, ask for someone to pick you up.

27. **Record every session you do**. Share the video on your blog and watch it yourself. Learn from it. This takes a single talk and makes it evergreen and scalable.

28. **Ask for testimonials.** Don't just assume the organizer will send one.

29. **Keep speaking**. Once you start speaking, you are going to want to keep those talks coming. Social media is a great tool for getting the word out. Share videos; get to know other speakers online. Learn about conferences and get out and attend them. "Speaking kits and demo reels are all well and good, but in my experience, it is all about contacts, personal brand, posturing and social proof to get booked at gigs."[6]

30. And last, worth saying twice at least: **It's not about you**. As with all parts of our businesses, let's remember to focus on what our audience or customers are looking for and be the one they look to when they need it.

---

[6]From Dean Hunt, http://deanhunt.com/the-best-advice-ever/.

30

Rocking a Panel

The whole is greater than the sum of its parts.

—Aristotle

I ASSUME ARISTOTLE was talking about a conference panel when he came up with this quote. That's what a panel should be: the discussion/content that is created is better than if each person was speaking on his or her own. Unfortunately, most panels I've seen rarely meet, let alone exceed, expectations.

In the last chapter, we talked about some tips for speakers. When you are part of a panel, all of those same tips are still important to pay attention to. Connecting with your audience before and after, showing your passion, not being tied to slides, and all the rest are critical to being the best possible part of a panel you can be.

Here are seven tips for making them worthwhile for everyone:

1. **Be an actual panel.** Four mini-presentations plus two minutes at the end for questions isn't a panel; it's four freaking presentations!

Allowing 10 minutes for each person to "present" isn't enough time to get into anything of substance, but take those away and open the entire session up for discussion . . . now we're onto something! So many panels talk about audience interaction and discussion, yet they leave only the last three minutes for audience questions and many people leave feeling unfulfilled. On the other side, I also don't think it should be left up to the audience entirely to ask the questions. The job of a great panel is to have a great discussion that naturally stimulates thought and questions from the audience.

2. **Have an actual moderator who moderates.** People like to hear themselves talk, *cough* me *cough,* but they can take over the panel. A good moderator not only knows how to cut off a blabbering mouth but also knows each person's strengths and can direct questions and rebuttals to the appropriate person. I sat on a panel next to a guy who said, "In my book, I talk about" seven times, and then at the end said, "Well, I guess I should mention my book" and held it up. I wanted to moderate him right in his nostril. The moderator should be on top of the self-promo, because that can kill a panel like nothing else.

3. **Have the moderator introduce each person.** This is one of my personal peeves. Either each panelist is allowed to tell the room about himself or herself or the moderator reads the prewritten bio. The issue is, given an open window, panelists can talk about themselves for 3 to 5 minutes each. This doesn't seem like much, but with four panelists and a moderator, introductions can last anywhere from 15 to 25 minutes! Most panels last for an hour total. I'd prefer the moderator, who sometimes picks who goes on the panel, to introduce each person with the reason that person was selected. Each introduction should be one minute, tops. I realize a lot of people speak on panels to get exposure for their company, but the best way to do this is to get into the meat of the panel topic and share great info.

4. **Stay on topic within reason.** This is also an issue with solo talks; the content doesn't match the description. It's even harder with multiple people on a panel. The biggest problem with not being related to the description is that people pick which concurrent session to attend based on that write-up, which means they aren't going to another. Especially for the huge events, such as BlogWorld,

SXSWi, PubCon, and Affiliate Summit, there are multiple tracks and topics. If you don't deliver on your promise, not only is there a letdown, but there's a missed opportunity to see another session that may have been more suitable.

5. **Don't use slides.** True, I'm in favor of banning them completely, but this is especially the case for a panel. It's a think tank, a place to create a dialog that happens nowhere else. A slide deck prevents this, especially if they're the same ones the panelists use in their individual presentations. Even when I'm on a panel that requires slides/minipresentations, I'll do something original for that panel, usually pulling up websites that have talking points for the panel topic (although this is dangerous, because it depends on usually unreliable conference Wi-Fi, but I'm a fan of living on the edge . . . or something).

6. **Include different opinions.** A real letdown for an audience is when each panelist says the same thing. This doesn't mean there has to be violent arguments, but you should have a different perspective on at least some points. On a BlogWorld panel I was on, my favorite part was when Shayne Tilley from SitePoint and I had different opinions on pop-ups. I said they were evil, and he said they worked. The discussion showed two passionate opinions, and I respect him for having it. To contrast this, during a panel at Canada 3.0, a policy writer from Google said, "People like reading ads" and I lost my mind—which was awesome. I don't think I'll be invited back, but I do love panels! Seriously, ask me to be on yours at any of the main conferences, and I'd jump faster than a kangaroo on Red Bull that has to pee.

7. **Ensure that the moderator knows each panelist.** I don't like it when conferences take it upon themselves to pair up moderators and panelists; I prefer the onus to be on the moderator to do his or her homework on the topic, participants, and audience. I recently went to an author panel to support some friends who were on it. Not only did the moderator not know who was on the panel, she even screwed up the introduction of half the panelists and failed to direct any questions of substance to the right panelist. And that easily, a potentially great panel was turned into a waste of time.

31

Shedding Some Social Pounds

When trying to convince somebody to be more social, you have to match the metric with the mind.

IN THE INTRODUCTION, one of the things I called on us all to do is to shed a few social pounds. Being awesome in business is not about being everywhere. The fewer resources we have, the harder it becomes to get the most out of our engagement online. Social media success is about being awesome where we are, not about being everywhere. This goes for our offline business lives as well. When your business begins to grow outside of what you yourself can manage, you need to let go of tasks and get some help. You are not scalable.

Unfortunately, we can all suffer from what I call social exhaustion. The big challenge with being authentic in social media is that it means you have to be in each of the online places you hang out. This isn't any more scalable than you in person. We are much less likely to see the windows of awesome that open up for us if we are just trying to keep up with being too many places online.

In my first book, I explained the concept of platforming and how you can choose the best places to start and grow your voice online. Basically, we all have a few choices to make:

- If you're part of a known brand, a brand that's being talked about on every platform, you have to either scale or optimize your listening. Picking only one platform doesn't help if people are raking you across the coals in four others. When it comes to responding, efficiency shouldn't be a part of your vocabulary. It needs to be personal, direct, and authentic.
- If you're an unknown brand and you want to create virtual momentum, pick a platform to start with. Make it an obsession for a fixed time frame. I don't care which one you decide to use. Facebook your heart out. Pinterest it up. Tweet your life. Just do it well. Do it to the point where if you're not there actively participating for a day, people e-mail you to ask you what's wrong.

The problem a lot of the time isn't convincing you to use it; it's that you have the job of convincing other people, be it your boss or a client. Saying a lot of people will "like" you or your brand doesn't fly with a lot of people in business, nor should it. When trying to convince somebody to be more social, you have to match the metric with the mind. This means you have to tell the other person what needle you're going to move, and then you have to move it. If you say it will increase sales, you'd better be able to show it can improve sales. If you say it can decrease calls into customer service, you better have the statistics to prove it. Pick a benchmark, measure it, and then be able to prove you can change it. Being against social media isn't stupid or bad business. Questioning anything that takes up time and resources for your company is actually good business.

Understand something: in 2008, no one had heard of me. I ran my company behind the scenes. Then, in January 2009, I decided to change all that by doing exactly this. A few book deals, a few hundred talks, and a boatload of awesome clients later, I think it works.

32

You Don't Need the Man If You Are the Man

Why I Love Louis CK

More and more gatekeepers need to become platforms.

WHEN WE'RE TALKING about taking our investment online and moving it forward to position ourselves as experts, we need to talk about content creation. In my first book, I spoke a lot about creating content and the how-tos of video and other media. What I want us to look at here is how creating and sharing are changing as the online world removes barriers and gatekeepers.

Louis CK made a lot of waves online in 2011 by bringing his newest comedy special direct to the public through his website. I'm a big fan of his; he's actually the funniest comedian I've ever seen. His decision to create, produce, market, and sell his own video special without the middleman and sell it direct to the customer for $5 per download was hugely successful.

Although $5 is a pittance of a price compared with the usual cost of a DVD comedy special, it sure added up. At $5 at a time,

200,000 times, the comedian brought in a quick million dollars. After covering the $250,000 in costs, dividing another $250,000 up with his crew, he then went on Twitter and asked fans for suggestions for charities to donate the next quarter million. For the last $250,000, he said, quite awesomely, it was none of our damn business; he would do with it as he pleased. But, he let his fans know that if he reached another million, he would divide it up again the same way.[1]

He put no restrictions on sharing the digital content, no digital rights management (DRM) to stop it from being shared freely. The only thing he said was one mention on his website about not being an asshole. It says right on the page that you are welcome to burn it to DVD. Not only did I give Louis my $5, I went back and bought two more "copies" to give to friends. The content was great, I loved how he made it so easy to watch and share, and the price was right.

This entire event created quite a stir in the marketing/social/online community. People were screaming that the establishment was dead and how we don't need networks or gatekeepers anymore.

But I disagree.

It is awesome what happened. It is awesome what's possible. But with fractional reaction, Louis CK had to reach millions online to get that number of sales. Without the huge media companies to help launch and grow his career, it would be much harder to get to this point, if even possible at all. This is not something that would work for a new comedian without a following. What it does show is that you can have success with a virtual product that is not locked down and guarded by gatekeepers.

The ability to create content directly for viewers has been around for a long time, on places such as YouTube, for example. But in their model, money is made from popular videos using advertising, not by selling the content. For the artist to be able to monetize the content, without selling ads, is a huge challenge. Louis CK proved that if you build a platform with great content, eventually you can sell something other than an ad, without giving away most (or all) of your content for free.

Sometimes making the controls on your content overbearing will hurt the content itself. I have seen everything from custom secure

---

[1] https://buy.louisck.net/news.

video players to issues facing e-books, such as custom readers and rules against printing copies. Some go as far as locking down content with passwords—this is content that has already been paid for. This is coming from an author.[2] If my worst problem is that this book is too easy to share, then I don't have much of a problem. If the price is fair and the content is great, people will buy.

The walls have been coming down, and a lot of the power and control of the middleman within creation is being removed. We see examples in record companies, book publishers, and movie houses. Although the barrier to creation and distribution has shrunk immensely, that does not mean we've lost the use for them. Whether these gatekeepers act as investors or distributors, or simply experts who understand their industries, there are still benefits to working with them.

I love the online world and how we all have more and more choices about what content works for us, but it is not as simple as yelling publishing or another industry is "dead" and thinking the layers between consumers and creators are no longer important or valuable. They are being eroded and changed, and people can go around them to find creations they love. More and more gatekeepers need to become platforms. They need to make their value about sharing and investment—in time and risk.

Once you have your own CK-style platform, maybe you won't need the gatekeepers anymore. But I think, until you do, undervaluing their investment is unwise. Many people have argued this point with me, but as my man Louis CK says, "Nobody ever wins an argument. Nobody ever goes, 'Oh, I'm wrong.' Somebody eventually just goes, 'Shut up. We gotta eat, so let's shut up for a minute.'"

---

[2]Duh . . . you're reading the book.

33

The Hall of Fame

Stop being afraid. Be first.

PEOPLE HAVE SAID that I focus too much on the evil happening in business, and I can't really disagree. There is just so much terrible customer service, so many people and companies tweeting and posting without thinking out there, that finding the bad online is like shooting fish in a barrel.

To be honest, though, the stories that resonate with me the most, and in turn with audiences I speak to around the world, are the awesome ones. We all crave good experiences with companies, and we all want to be good examples ourselves.

When looking through all the examples of awesome I have run across, it strikes me that there is a direct correlation between how awesome something is and how little we expect it to be. We spend too much time worrying about trying something new in business. The truly awesome happens when we take risks. Stop being afraid. Be first.

The less awesome the industry, the product, or the job is, the more impactful even the smallest thing can be. You will see here—with all of our Hall of Fame inductees—that it does not require a big budget, a fancy position, or the shiniest product to be mind-blowingly awesome at what you do. You just have to want to be awesome.

These examples are all of people who, just like you and me, have opportunities to be awesome every day. Little windows open up but can close very quickly. They just decided that today was the day—which turned into their big moment, for them and their customers.

As you read through the examples, you will find some common themes. If you want to join the ranks in this hallowed hall, all you really need to do is be authentic, make it personal, and make your customers feel amazing about their choice to do business with you.

For updates and more stories about the Awesome Hall of Fame, visit www.TheBookOfBusinessAwesome.com/HallOfFame.

34

Mr. Happy Crack

What's your excuse for not being awesome again?

BEING AWESOME IN BUSINESS has nothing to do with which industry you're in; it's actually easier to be awesome in industries you never thought it was possible in because the bar has been set so low. Nothing defines that better than this nominee to the Business Awesome Hall of Fame: the Crack Team.

The Crack Team describes themselves online like this:[1]

Since 1985 The Crack Team has specialized in foundation repair and waterproofing. For 25 years we've been providing permanent and cost-effective solutions to one of the biggest problems facing homeowners: cracked and leaking concrete. From crack repair to sump pumps to structural solutions, The Crack Team has the experience and the knowledge to solve your foundation-related problems. Plus, our lifetime-of-the-structure "Happy Crack

---

[1] http://www.thecrackteam.com/.

Guarantee" gives you the peace of mind you want. When it's repaired by The Crack Team, it's repaired forever.

You can tell right away that they aren't letting their industry get in the way of their awesome. They didn't look to competitors to define their brand or dictate what could or should be done for their business. I learned about the Crack Team and Mr. Happy Crack from Petri Darby (@darbyDarnit on Twitter). He wrote about the company on his blog here:[2]

With brilliant marketing and a fresh, hip image, this foundation repair business is quickly making a name for itself as an up and coming franchise. People are actively seeking to purchase hats, umbrellas, shirts and other paraphernalia featuring the company's mascot/logo "Mr. Happy Crack," and many of its customers are demanding that they receive such items with their service. Now that is brand evangelism.

And again here:[3]

In an earlier blog column, I wrote about a seemingly boring franchise concept—a foundation repair business (I know, YAWN, right?)—that was turned on its head through simple, focused, and buzzworthy branding.

Well, after I sang the company's praises, I received a package in the mail with a shirt, stickers, keychains, and an autographed portrait of the organization's mascot, Mr. Happy Crack, along with a note that said "Flattery gets you everywhere." The Crack Team actually thanks those who help further its message and interests—imagine that.

Are you missing out on an opportunity to turn your audience into advocates, even raging fans? And when they provide you with free, valuable word-of-mouth referrals, do you thank them and demonstrate your appreciation? I can't tell you how many people I've told about The Crack Team. I don't know if they have an

---

[2]http://bit.ly/CrackTeam1.
[3]http://bit.ly/CrackTeam2.

external PR, marketing and/or advertising partner, but that is the type of client I dream about. Doing well by doing good. Keep up the stellar work.

I happen to own a Mr. Happy Crack doll myself. I mean, how could I not? I show the mascot's image in talks around the world, and every single time I show him, the audience goes bananas. Not just because their slogan is "a dry crack is a happy crack" but because it is so unexpected and so awesome. Being amazing to a market that isn't expecting it isn't harder; it's easier. You just have to see the window and go for it.

Have a look at Mr. Happy Crack (see Figure 34.1) one more time and remind me, what's your excuse for not being awesome again?

Figure 34.1   The Awesome Mr. Happy Crack

35

Pimp My Lift

So what kind of products do you sell again that can't be awesome?

SOMETIMES THERE ARE PRODUCTS that just do not lend themselves to the awesome realm. Commodities, everyday things, and even machinery—they don't exactly get people jumping on their Share button when they see it. This nominee for the Awesome Hall of Fame, MasterLift Forklifts, a manufacturer of forklifts (Really what else would they make with a name like that?) in my town of Oakville, Ontario, decided unawesome was unacceptable and created PimpMyLift.ca.

Taking the name from the popular *Pimp My Ride* TV show, visitors to the site could "pimp out" their own personal forklifts. You wanna black forklift with orange flames screaming up the side? You got it! Want sweet rims? Done! Then everyone could share the picture of his or her lifts online. And, here's the kicker, you could actually buy your own custom forklift.

How's this for the ROI of being awesome? They canceled their Yellow Pages ad and put the money toward this new site and had exponentially higher results, selling nine forklifts when it was launched, which is a huge number for an industrial machinery company of their size.

I'm not sure what your awesome will be. That's one of the problems with looking at what other people and companies are doing and trying to learn from them. You need to find your own way, your own personality, and your own voice. Too often we try to take the easy way out and mimic others, rather than being ourselves. Remember when you read about these nominees that they are meant to inspire, not be copied. What makes these companies great is how they embraced their uniqueness and created something unexpected.

One of the best things about this awesome nominee is that their viral reach was outside of their target market but spread within their market as well. You don't need to make a purchase to create your own personal folklift. See, I made one myself (see Figure 35.1)!

So what kind of products do you sell again that can't be awesome? I think you need to rethink that.

Figure 35.1   The UnForkLift

36

Nightmares

Be prepared for your success.

THERE ARE NOT MANY THINGS I fear in life: red jeans, asparagus-flavored gum, and haunted houses (I won't set foot in them, because they scare the crap out of me). However, I must admit that a fantastic example of taking a locally based awesome experience and sharing it virtually is Nighmares Fear Factory, a haunted house in Niagara Falls, Ontario.

I've asked Elizabeth Monier-Williams to share her breakdown of this awesomeness for the book. Mostly, because I am scared to check it out further myself. Seriously, check out this photo of people inside the place (Figure 36.1).

I don't know what they're seeing, but I know I don't want to see it. As for me, I am not likely to visit Nightmares Fear Factory. Given my track record with horror movies, I would probably get a Chicken Card three feet through the door.

For some other great thoughts check out the rest of Elizabeth's blog at www.theanalyticeye.com.

Figure 36.1   Capturing People at Their Worst Is the Best

Source: Nightmares Fear Factory, Niagara Falls, Canada.
NightmaresFearFactory.com. Used with permission.

5 Viral Takeaways from Nightmares Fear Factory

When Vee Popat arrived at work on Thursday, October 6, 2011, everything seemed normal. Near mid-day, he checked the analytics for the website and social media accounts he maintains as director of sales and marketing for Nightmares Fear Factory, a haunted house and tourist attraction located in Niagara Falls, Ontario.

Instead of the usual pattern of approximately 600 unique visits per day, his website traffic had doubled. Curious, Popat did some digging. Over 700 visits had come from two referring sites in particular: first from BuzzFeed.com and then a message board. After lunch, another 1,500 hits arrived courtesy of Tumblr. Shortly after that, the media started calling. By the end of the day, Nightmares Fear Factory had received 60,000 unique visits—a one-day increase of 10,000 percent.

Popat watched the numbers climb, experiencing a certain degree of disbelief as his communications strategy achieved what many social media and marketing experts promise and few deliver.

Nightmares Fear Factory had just gone viral.

(continued)

(continued)

Last week, my brother did what thousands of people have done all over the world this October. He sent me a link to Nightmares Fear Factory's Flickr stream, which features hilarious photographs of people touring the haunted house. Most of the visitors, photographed by hidden cameras during the experience, are clearly losing their minds

Since the BuzzFeed groundswell, Nightmares' website, photos, and social media pages have attracted worldwide coverage.

A quick glance through their Twitter feed provides an impressive media pedigree: the *Toronto Star*, *ABC News*, *Good Morning America*, the *Huffington Post*, the *Wall Street Journal*, *Canada AM*, and Digg.com, among others. They also got a shout out from Jay Leno on *The Tonight Show*. Beyond the obvious appeal of funny photographs, what can this Internet sensation teach communicators, marketers, and social media strategists about creating a viral campaign?

I contacted Popat and we spoke about Nightmares' social media strategy and how he optimized their content for global success.

Here are the five key points to take away from Nightmares Fear Factory's example:

1. Generate smart, cohesive content that builds your brand in core directions.
2. Always use social media to engage your existing audience first.
3. Look for piggyback opportunities, but make sure your message is highly shareable.
4. Be patient. Success is rarely achieved overnight.
5. Protect what makes you unique.

1. Generate Smart, Cohesive Content

Creating a strong social media campaign is impossible without having equally strong conventional marketing backing it up.

What immediately struck me about Nightmares Fear Factory is how adept they are at integrating social media with their existing web content. Their website has the kind of aesthetic you would expect for a haunted house: disturbing photos that allude to gore without actually showing it, fonts that look like blood smears, and creepy music (big plus—you can turn the music off).

Beneath the window dressing, all the basics you would expect for a tourist attraction are thoroughly covered: directions and maps, hours, pricing, group rates, a FAQs page, and so on.

Better still, their site features:

- Three versions—static HTML, mobile, and Flash—so that visitors can choose the browsing experience best suited to their needs.
- Online ticket purchasing, including discounts for buying online in advance and specific options for mobile phone users.
- Clear explanations of how the safe word process works for visitors who find the experience too overwhelming to continue.
- A 13 percent discount for buying tickets online along with other contests.

Social media links are fully integrated with this content at logical points. Highlights include:

- Buttons for Twitter, Facebook, YouTube, and Flickr, where the brand presence is continued using complementary layouts. All four channels feature current content, which is impressive since Popat maintains all social channels himself (he does get support work where needed from Charlie Montney II and Taylor Toth, the Web developer and graphic designer/video producer who work with him on the main site, respectively).
- Modified buttons for the mobile site, including Foursquare and Gowalla. When I asked why they don't include those

(continued)

(*continued*)

buttons on the main site, Popat said they decided people were unlikely to check in to location-based social media platforms using desktop computers, which strikes me as a fair assumption.

- Links to Yelp and Trip Advisor among their social media button set. I had never seen buttons like these before, but they make a lot of sense for a small business that is also a tourist attraction. The practice also speaks to the company's commitment to transparency in its communications and willingness to listen to user feedback (judging by my quick tour of websites for Canada's Wonderland, the Royal Ontario Museum, Toronto Zoo, Ontario Science Centre, and Ontario Place, this best practice makes Nightmares Fear Factory fairly unique among Greater Toronto Area attractions).
- Their Facebook page allows you to buy tickets online without visiting the main site and to leave reviews.
- YouTube videos that are integrated with the Facebook page.
- A Twitter background that makes use of the best Flickr photos.
- Two photo galleries on the main website (Fear Pics of the Day; Top 10 Pics of the Week) that both include links to the Facebook account.
- A video gallery on the main website that takes visitors directly to the Nightmares Fear Factory's YouTube page. Popat explained this is a recent change since the media interest they received crashed their original server and forced an overhaul for how their site handles video. Changing from streaming video to YouTube redirects was a contingency plan to reduce the load on their server, but Popat anticipates that embedded YouTube videos will replace streaming video on their pages as they complete the website overhaul.

Why is all this detail significant? Because when Nightmares Fear Factories' 15 seconds of fame arrived, they had the structural underpinning in place via their web and social media presence to support and direct the traffic surge in meaningful ways. And that speaks to the insight of their strategy.

2. Engage Your Existing Audience First

When I started researching this post, one of the things I liked best about Nightmares Fear Factory is the clear distinction between their Facebook and Twitter accounts.

Both feeds are celebratory, engaged, and feature similar content, but the wording and tone are different, implying that a real human is doing the posting in both places.

Popat confirmed that he has read the same articles I have about why it's worth it to make your Twitter and Facebook streams different:

> When we were planning the strategy, I felt Twitter and Facebook speak to different audiences who respond in different ways to content. So while the links, photos, or video are often the same, the words or tone referring people to them are different. I try to change it up and keep both platforms fresh.

What immediately stands out about both feeds—both before and after the viral surge—is that they are used to engaging with prospective, recent, and longtime visitors and fans.

When I viewed the Nightmares Twitter feed on October 16, 2011, it included plenty of @ messages. I haven't done a scientific study, but Popat seems to follow Scott Stratten's[1] (@unmarketing) rule that you should reply on Twitter far more often than you plug your own material.

Some tweets shared media mentions, directly answered visitor concerns (including one that was clearly about a complaint), or acknowledged related blog postings by Nightmares fans.

(continued)

---

[1] That guy does sound like a genius. . . .

(*continued*)

On Facebook, the conversation is similar. Popat posts about contests, new photos, and the like, but also acknowledges fan requests to get survivor photos, be named Survivor of the Week, and for other general information.

Their Facebook page also includes likes for other Niagara region attractions, which is good online citizenship for a tourism-focused business. More important, for every post Popat makes to the Nightmares Facebook wall, there is at least one from another Facebook user—and almost every single one had a reply from Popat.

As I mentioned earlier, the Nightmares Fear Factory Facebook presence is robust enough that visitors can research the attraction, plan a visit, and buy tickets without needing to visit the main site.

Taken collectively, these elements demonstrate an understanding of the user experience and a willingness to put guest convenience ahead of pushing traffic to a central site.

I wonder how many other tourist attractions can make the same claim.

3. Look for Piggyback Opportunities

It does not shock me that Nightmares Fear Factory's explosive popularity came in October, two weeks before Halloween—a time when every features editor, morning show producer, and topical website in North America is looking for new content to put a fresh spin on the holiday. Nightmares Fear Factory's content is an excellent tie-in for Halloween coverage—scary, funny, and something you can actually do if you live near or can travel to Niagara Falls.

Most important, their ready-made content (photos, video, etc.) makes talking about their story incredibly easy for time-challenged producers and reporters. And with strong brand integration on a variety of social media channels, it's easy for the people reading mainstream coverage to become brand messengers by sharing content within their personal networks.

Popat has also covered his conventional bases by writing a press release about the viral phenomenon, along with contact information. The press release was made readily available on the Nightmares site when it became clear some kind of official statement was needed.

4. Be Patient. Success Is Rarely Achieved Overnight

Looking at photos of people losing their minds in a haunted house is a perfect combination of hilarity, voyeurism, and fun—and advertising. But the media firestorm didn't come during their first Halloween in the social media landscape; Nightmares Fear Factory has been on Facebook for two years and Flickr for a year.

BuzzFeed.com is essentially a cool-hunting service that allows users to submit ideas and predict what will go viral and what won't. Popat acknowledged he had never heard of BuzzFeed before it amplified his traffic to kingdom come; he's not sure who exactly decided to pick up Nightmares Fear Factory's photos and make them the Internet's newest cool kid.

The lesson is clear, though: you can have the best content in the world, but it *still* takes a lot of time and effort for the right people to find your material.

And although hindsight is 20/20, it's hard to tell exactly who needs to see your stuff for your content to go viral.

5. Protect What Makes You Unique

The biggest question Popat gets from visitors, reporters, and social media friends alike is the obvious one: What the hell are those people looking at in the photos?

There is a certain genius in Nightmare Fear Factory's decision to focus exclusively on the faces of their terrified guests. On some level, it doesn't matter what is scaring them. Young or old, men or women, the photos show humanity at its most wigged-out.

Notices advising visitors that they will be photographed and/or recorded are present in both the lobby and on the website.

(continued)

(*continued*)

Visitors can also sign a waiver for photography and video before they enter, but the photos tend to be a pride point for guests.

Popat often receives messages asking, "Can you post my picture?" or "Can I be the Survivor of the Week?" Many visitors think Nightmares staff post all the photos, but there are too many (and not all of them are funny). They will take down individual photos if someone complains. As Popat explains, "We're not posting them to embarrass people."

Summing Up

Although social media often feels like it functions completely at the level of instant gratification, the truth is that true overnight Internet sensations are built with time, energy, and effort. It's something all marketers and communicators should keep in mind when trying to secure more resources or sell a direct report on the ROI of a new campaign.

Nightmares Fear Factory demonstrates that a strong connection between regular and social media marketing can yield huge payoffs, but only if you're willing to commit the time and energy to doing it right.

Source: Elizabeth Monier-Williams, "5 Viral Takeaways from Nightmare Fear Factory." © November 2, 2011. http://theanalyticeye.com/2011/10/5-viral -takeaways-from-nightmares-fear-factory/. Used with permission.

I love a lot of things about this social success story. But for me, the take home is that it is an example of great content going viral with time, commitment, and great overall management and setup. They knew the idea was awesome, they stuck with it, and they set it up for success. So when the world caught on to what they were up to, they were ready. Going viral and getting more attention than you're prepared to harness and manage might as well not happen at all. When you get all those views and visits, you need to be ready to do something about them; otherwise, why bother at all?

Learn from Nightmares and be prepared for your success.

37

An Awesome Sweatband

Opportunities to engage with our fans are windows of awesome.

THESE NOMINEES PROVE that just because most people know you, it doesn't mean you can't still touch one person at a time. Opportunities are everywhere to acknowledge fans, followers, and customers. Whether it's pen to paper, face-to-face, or virtual, we all have the ability to create unforgettable moments with our fans—moments they will share.

Our first example, the old-school handwritten kind, comes to us from J.K. Rowling (you may have heard of her). She and I are both authors.[1] Sure she's sold a few more books than I have—okay, a lot more books. She is phenomenally popular, to the point where the world makes demands on time every minute of the day.

So when a young fan named Sacia Flowers wrote to her, sharing how much J.K.'s writing meant in her life, we might expect

---

[1]She just writes about wizards, whereas I write about jackasses and unicorns.

the letter to go unnoticed, or even undelivered. But that's not what happened at all. Sacia received a personal note back from J.K. herself (http://www.lettersofnote.com/2011/07/i-will-treasure-your-letter.html). The letter was written so wonderfully, you feel as if J.K. herself is standing there with her hand on Sacia's shoulder, speaking right to her.[2]

I'm pretty sure that if an individual as well known and as busy as J.K. Rowling is has time to answer a fan letter, then we all can reply to a tweet. I'm sure she could have ignored the letter without its affecting sales or her newest book. I doubt the letter was written with the intent of increased revenue. She did not need to consider the ROI of replying to a fan.

Online fan engagement should be a no-brainer. If someone posts or tweets about you or your brand, product, or service, a simple thank you can make that person's day. This is one of the reasons listening to what people are saying about our brands is so important. Too often, the negative voices get all of our attention, when we should be focusing on the positive as well. When I get a tweet about my book, it's an opportunity to high-five a fan when that person is holding his or her hand in the air. Leaving your fans hanging is not only awkward, it can be embarrassing for them, to the point where people can turn on you if you never acknowledge them.

An example of face-to-face fan appreciation that really stuck with me happened recently when I attended a New York Knicks game at Madison Square Garden. I'm not really a Knicks fan, but I am a huge sports fan and I love seeing events in cities I visit. At the end of what was an amazing game, a kid ran up to the railing where the players walked off the court and pleaded for something, anything from a player—a high-five, a fist bump, even a smile. You could tell by the way the seven-year-old watched the players pass by that these were his idols, and none of them were giving him the time of day. Then Baron Davis walked by and handed the kid his sweatband.

I saw it happen, and my grown-up brain thought that was pretty cool of him. It wasn't until I saw the child again with his dad as I was walking upstairs to leave the game that I realized the impact of

---

[2]Not to mention, if she ever got teased again at school, she could turn to them and say, "I'm sorry. I didn't hear you. I was reading my letter from J.K. Freakin' Rowling."

what Davis had given him. His dad was taking his picture as he stood shaking and wearing the biggest smile on his face that I'd ever seen. He had this look of amazement on his face, like he'd flown in an F-15 that had just done 10 barrel rolls. Shaking and smiling and saying over and over, "I got Baron Davis's headband." While every other player had just walked by him, this little token literally changed the child's brain and will no doubt make him a Knicks fan for life.

Encounters with people we admire can leave impressions that last a lifetime. How people of status react to fans, whether an author, an athlete, or a musician, can affect the person's opinion of their entire body of work. No doubt, opportunities to engage with our fans are windows of awesome. Whether a simple appreciation or thank you tweeted to me about my book, all the way up to a shaking child wearing Baron Davis's sweatband, fans are a privilege to have and should be treated as such. Not that I'm comparing myself to Baron Davis or any other of the New York Knicks.[3]

Sure, I'm not J.K. Rowling, and you're probably not Baron Davis.[4] But we are all something to somebody. Whether that somebody is the new entry-level kid right out of college in our department or a customer on Facebook who just wants to say thank you, we make impressions on minds, or depressions in brands, depending on how we react. There is no such thing as a neutral reaction. The few seconds it takes to send back a "thanks," answer a question, or even send a smile is really all our fans and customers are looking for.

---

[3] Although Patrick Ewing and I have the same number of NBA championship rings. Hey-oo!

[4] Unless you are Baron Davis, in which case, hey man, what's up? I was just kidding about that Patrick Ewing thing.

38

Moncton Snowblower

This is my snowblower. Make it your snowblower.

FOR OUR NEXT NOMINEE, I'm electing this ad that appeared on Kijiji for a snowblower.[1] I'm sure you're thinking to yourself, "Come on now, Scott, a used snowblower on a free ad site? How awesome can that be?"

And that is exactly the problem and why they deserve to be here. There are so many ads out there, you have to cut through the clutter to ensure that yours gets seen. The ad printed here was not only seen, and successfully sold the product, but went crazy online and received international media attention. This guy took what could have been a pitch a few lines long and punched all the other ads in the throat.

---

[1] http://bit.ly/SnowBlower.

Check it out:

Some Long Overdue Kijiji Action

Do you like shoveling snow? Then stop reading this and go back to your pushups and granola because you are not someone that I want to talk to.

Let's face it, we live in a place that attracts snow like Magnetic Hill attracts cars, only that ain't an illusion out there. That's 12 inches of snow piling up and, oh, what's that sound? Why it's the snowplow and it's here to let you know that it hates you and all the time you spent to shovel your driveway. Did you want to get out of your house today? Were you expecting to get to work on time? Or even this week?

You gave it your best shot. You tried to shovel by yourself and I respect you for that. I did it, my parents did it, some of my best friends did it. But deep down inside, we all wanted to murder that neighbor with the snowblower who has finished and on his second beer while you were still trying to throw snow over a snowbank taller than you are.

So, here we are. You could murder your neighbour, which could ensure that you won't need to shovel a driveway for 25 to life, but there are downsides to that too. What to do?

Here's the deal. I have a snowblower and you want to own it. I can tell you're serious about this. It's like I can almost see you: sitting there, your legs are probably crossed and your left hand is on your chin. Am I right? How'd I do that? The same way that I know that YOU ARE GOING TO BUY THIS SNOWBLOWER.

I want you to experience the rush that comes with smashing through a snowdrift and blowing that mother trucker out of the way. The elation of seeing the snowplow come back down your street and watching the look of despair as your OTHER neighbour gets his shovel out once more while you kick back with a hot cup of joe (you don't have a drinking problem like that other guy).

Here's what you do. You go to the bank. You collect $900. You get your buddy with a truck and you drive over here. You

(continued)

(*continued*)

give me some cold hard cash and I give you a machine that will mess up a snowbank sumthin' fierce. I've even got the manual for it, on account of I bought it brand new and I don't throw that kind of thing away. Don't want to pay me $900? Convince me. Send me an offer and I'll either laugh at you and you'll never hear back from me or I'll counter.

You want a snowblower. You need a snowblower.

This isn't some entry level snowblower that is just gonna move the snow two feet away. This is an 11 HP Briggs and Stratton machine of snow doom that will cut a 29 inch path of pure ecstasy. And its only four years old. I dare you to find a harder working four year old. My niece is five and she gets tired and cranky after just a few minutes of shoveling. This guy just goes and goes and goes.

You know what else? I greased it every year to help keep the water off it and the body is in as good shape as possible. It's greasier than me when I was 13, and that's saying something.

You know how many speeds it has? Six forward and two in reverse. It goes from "leisurely" slow up to "light speed." Seriously, I've never gone further than five because it terrifies me. I kid you not, you could probably commute to work with it dragging you.

You know what else is crappy about clearing snow in the morning? That you have to do it in the dark. Well, not anymore! It has a halogen headlight that will light your way like some kind of moveable lighthouse (only better, because lighthouses won't clear your driveway).

Oh, and since it's the 21st century this snowblower comes with an electric starter. Just plug that sucker in, push the button, and get ready to punch snow in the throat. If you want to experience what life was like in the olden days, it comes with a back-up cord you could pull to start it, but forget that. The reason you're getting this fearsome warrior was for the convenience, so why make it harder on yourself?

By this point, you're probably wondering why I would sell my snowblower since the first snowpocalypse is upon us today.

I'll tell you why: because I heard it was time for you to man up and harness some mighty teeth and claws and chew your way to freedom, that's why.

This is my snow blower. Make it your snow blower.

Update—I assure you that the snowblower is real and it is still available. Do not despair if you have made an offer on this glorious tribute to man's triumph over nature and I have not responded yet, your time has yet to come.

Update 2—It appears someone feels they have the courage to harness this snow siege weapon and blaze a divine path for all to follow this winter. Snowblower is sold, pending pick up.

Source: Weh-Ming Cho, "Some Long Overdue Kijiji Action." © 2001. http://www.blognostifier.com/2011/11/some-long-overdue-kijiji-action.html. Used with permission.

Tell me you don't want to buy that snowblower now, either. I don't even need a snowblower, and I want to buy it. I tried to pick just a few lines from the ad to show you, but it was impossible to choose. There are 1,000 snowblowers for sale on Kijiji; only one got this kind of media attention. According to the ad writer himself, 48,574 people linked to the ad via Facebook. He received a ton of attention because of the ad, including job offers. I can see why. I want to hire him, don't you? This was written without an ad agency, a copywriter, or committees. Obviously this guy has natural talent. When he was asked about the ad and how crazy things went online he responded, "In the last 72 hours, I believe I have had a total of 10 hours of sleep—being Internet Famous is exhausting." How awesome is that?

There are countless other examples online of ads like this, for roommates, concrete bricks, and other mundane boring things. The nature of what you are trying to sell is not an excuse for a boring ad. Some personality, and a little bit of snowblower-type attitude, can transform the same boring thing everyone else is selling into something amazing. Sometimes we filter out the awesome in business, believing we need big budgets and huge platforms before we start being awesome.

But I disagree. I think we can all start today.

39

Calgary Philharmonic

Truly being awesome in a sometimes unawesome space.

SOMETIMES BEING AWESOME is doing the exact opposite of what your industry does. This nominee to the Hall of Fame, from Calgary, Alberta, shows us that you can be awesome by having a little fun by going against the grain of your industry.

Looking for a creative way to promote their city online, Tourism Calgary went on Twitter and asked their followers to reply with their best tips for staying warm in the winter. Tons of people tweeted back, and they chose the best answers and created an epic choir video.[1]

In the video, the Calgary Philharmonic Orchestra Choir sing the replies set to the tune of Carmina Burana's piece, "O Fortuna." Some of the lines included "Hunker down and find your mittens" and "Make some really good mulled wine."

More than 100,000 views later, they have reached a whole new audience and brand awareness in Canada and around the world. The

---

[1]You don't hear that phrase very often.

video was created by the Canadian agency Village&Co. When asked about its creation, this is what they had to say:

> As Tourism Calgary's Social Media Agency of Record we are in tune with the city's social landscape. Calgary has a very social media savvy population and we saw a creative opportunity to engage with that community.[2]

I love how the agency recognized that their market used social media and brought that together with the amazing resource of such a talented orchestra and choir. In the arts, Twitter or any kind of mobile phone use is usually frowned upon, both for marketing and when it comes to performances. Their bold move, along with some other theaters that are starting to promote mobile-friendly sections during performances, are truly being awesome in a sometimes unawesome space.

You can feel the passion for their art and their city come across in the video; it's full of fun and personality. You watch it and then want to share it, but not only that—you want to go. If passion and personality are unprofessional and wrong in your industry, then I want you out of that profession. Even in the world of mundane products, even in industries where showing personality is not the norm, there is room to be awesome. I want you to be the one to show the rest of your competitors how it can be done. Just like Calgary did.[3]

---

[2]http://bit.ly/CalgaryOrchestra.
[3]http://bit.ly/CalgaryTweets.

40

A Unicorn Fighting a Bear

UnAwesome is UnAcceptable.

AND NOW LADIES AND GENTLEMAN, our champion of the Business Awesome Hall of Fame. I don't care where you work or what your position is. To be awesome, all you need is a window of opportunity and apparently a Post-it Note.

This story starts out with John, a hungry fellow in Austin, Texas, ordering a pizza online. Now, when I order a pizza online, or any food for that matter, there is always a box at the end that asks for any additional comments or suggestions. I never know what to put in there. Maybe I should tell them that I like soup? I'm just not sure. John decided to be a smart-ass and requested the location draw a picture of a unicorn fighting a bear on the box.

I'm sure he did this to see if they were even reading it. Well, Chad, from the Austin's Pizza Call Center, saw this as his opportunity to be awesome. Seriously, what job do you have that can't be awesome when an assistant call center manager for a pizza place can be?

He decided to send the reply shown in Figure 40.1.

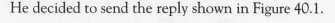

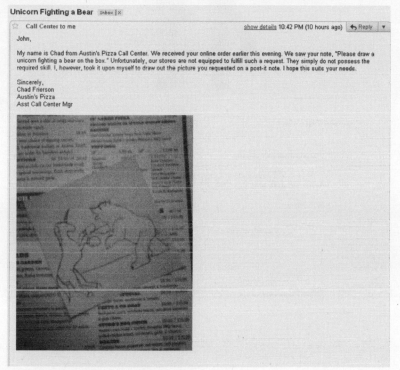

Figure 40.1   A Unicorn Boxing a Bear

Note: In case you can't read the e-mail in Figure 40.1, here's what it says:
My name is Chad from Austin's Pizza Call Center. We received your online order earlier this evening. We saw your note, "Please draw a unicorn fighting a bear on the box." Unfortunately, our stores are not equipped to fulfill such a request. They simply do not possess the required skill. I, however, took it upon myself to draw out the picture you requested on a post-it note. I hope this suits your needs.

Needless to say this is the greatest thing of all time. John uploaded the picture to display its awesomeness, which then went viral and was seen by millions of people. This story reigns supreme over all others, not just because it includes a unicorn, although that certainly helps. This was done by somebody in a frontline position with seemingly little autonomy, at no cost to the company, in an industry not known for being mind-blowing. It was done with immediacy and personality, without focus groups or a meeting beforehand. He did not run back and form a committee to deal with the unique request. He simply decided that unawesome is unacceptable, saw the window and acted on the awesome, and his action was rewarded with millions of views.

41

Awesome End

We need to look for those windows of opportunity every day.

THE HURDLES TO BEING AWESOME aren't that high. You just have to want to do it. Maybe millions won't see your act, but even if you move just one customer from static to ecstatic, you've made a huge difference and it's worth it. You can make your job a little more personally fulfilling. We simply need to decide that UnAwesome is UnAcceptable. We need to look for those windows of opportunity every day and stop making excuses because of our product, our industry, our position, or the amount of money we have on hand to move us forward.

For those of you who started reading this book from the Awesome side, take off your rose-colored glasses and flip over to the UnAwesome side. Hold on tight and get ready to enjoy the ride in contrast.

For the pessimist, who started on the UnAwesome side and has now begrudgingly finished here, good on ya. You're now done with the

Awesome, UnAwesome journey. Pop on over to TheBookOfBusiness-Awesome.com to see updates, read more stories of business awesome, and share your own. I will eventually be writing a third book, and I'm going to need material. I'm spent. Heck, I had to really, really, really, really, really, really stretch to meet the word count for this one. Really. Shoot me an e-mail at awesome@un-marketing.com, or say hi on Twitter anytime: @unmarketing.

The Book of Business **UnAwesome**

The Book of Business **UnAwesome**

The Cost of Not Listening, Engaging, or Being Great at What You Do

Scott Stratten

Author of UnMarketing

WILEY

John Wiley & Sons, Inc.

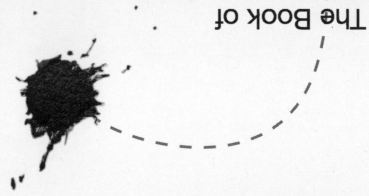

Contents

UnAwesome Acknowledgments

Inspired by "Here's to the Misfits" campaign for Apple.

HERE'S TO the jackasses.

The annoying salespeople. To the marketers who think being offensive is funny and any press is good press.

To the haters who couldn't stand the first book, because of the footnotes, the tone, or the fake testimonials on the back.

To the trolls online who make every great person look even better.

To the ones who have always told the rest of us that we couldn't do it, because you have reaffirmed the thought that we damn well can.

And even though I tell people not to be the Jackass Whisperer, I am going to whisper this to you. Without you, this half of the book wouldn't exist. And without you, everybody would be great at what they did, and therefore greatness wouldn't exist.

This book is for you.

1

Usually High Call Volume

What we do trumps what we say every time.

I HAVE TO CALL MY BANK a lot. Because of all the travelling I do, they like me to keep in touch about where I am. You know, to make sure those withdrawals in Vegas one day, lunch out at home a few days later, and then a taxi in Chicago the next week are all on the up-and-up. I would check up on me, too.

Now they always say their mission is customer satisfaction. In fact, my bank's number one core value, as listed on their website, is to "Deliver Legendary Customer Experiences." Legendary. You see that and you know that you are important to them. The customer *is* the bank.

The problem is, when I call, I get this message while I wait for my legendary customer service experience: "We are experiencing unusually high call volumes." You expect this sometimes, right? I get it; we're all busy. The thing is, for the past five years, every single time I call, I hear this message. And I got to wondering, when exactly

do unusually high call volumes become the usual high call volumes? There is no such thing as a 24-hour-long peak time for calls.

They say that the customer is most important, that service is number one, but they act differently. You are treated as though you aren't important at all. If I were really number one, they would staff their phone line properly. They would make it easier for me to use their services around the world. There would be no hoops, or at least very few, for me to jump through.

It usually costs a pretty penny for someone to write a company's mission statement, find a frame that's just right, and hang it on the wall. But if your actions contradict those values hanging on your wall or posted on your website, I suggest not investing in a nice frame, because the statement is worthless. In fact, you are no longer going to be writing your mission statement—because your customer is going to rewrite it for you. What we do trumps what we say every time.

Welcome to *The Book of Business UnAwesome*, where we look at the ways businesses are letting us down, messing things up, and of course, causing the brand train wrecks we can't take our eyes off of. We're going to look at UnAwesome in all areas of business, from marketing and public relations (PR) to human resources (HR) and customer service.

Put on your seat belt, hold on tight, and get ready for a bumpy ride.

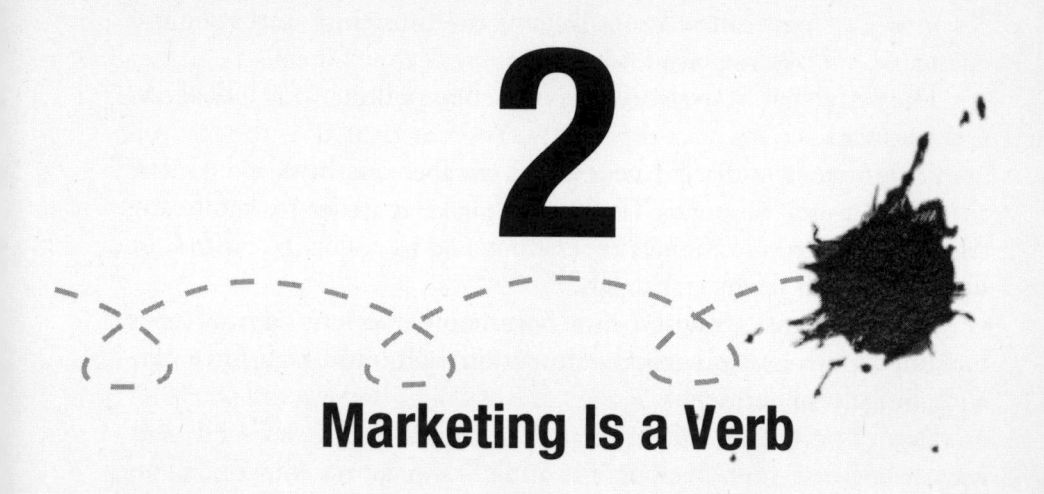

Marketing Is a Verb

It's what we do that affects our brand perception more than any brochure ever could.

WELCOME TO THE UNAWESOME SIDE.

You are the person who cheered on Darth Vader. You have Boba Fett statues in your office and Predator ones, too (just like I do). Don't be shy, UnAwesome reader; this is the side of the book I would read first, too.

It's not so much that we hate people. It's just that we've found, through experience and extensive research, that they're morons about 85 percent of the time.

You are the person who has been so abused as a customer for so long that even mediocre customer service feels extraordinary. You've had every kind of bad boss and horrible employee. And if one more of your friends invites you to vote for them, asks you to like their Facebook page, or reminds you about their LinkedIn request, you may just throw this book at them. You aren't expecting the awesome to happen, so you find yourself here, with me, on the UnAwesome side.

3

If you are in business yourself, here are the steps for creating the ultimate UnAwesome business.

The first step is to spend all of your money on brochures, billboards, and car wraps.

Place that order for Frisbees with your logo on them and a giant Yellow Pages ad. Be sure to have nothing left over to properly hire any talent whatsoever: no money for customer service, quality control, or the person who cleans up the lunchroom once a week.

Make sure your website is a non-mobile-friendly copy of your brochure. Flash is always good. Animations and music that force play automatically are critical.

Don't forget to include a pop up, pop in, and pop under—all great ways to increase your chances of beating that prospect who landed on your page over the head a few more times. Why not? They were just leaving, anyway.

Ignore your customers. Pretend the conversations they are having about you, online and offline, aren't happening at all. Really, wouldn't business be so much better if we didn't have to deal with pesky customers at all? The only time we should be reaching out to our market is with promotions and new product launches.

With these simple steps you are ready to go. Let the UnAwesome begin!

Serious Scott: I hope you can see how insanely ludicrous this all sounds, yet sadly this is exactly what you are doing when you think marketing is all about branding, brochures, and billboards. Marketing is a verb; it's what we do that affects our brand perception more than any brochure ever could. In the upcoming sections you are going to see how companies' actions speak louder than any printed word.

I cannot even begin to estimate how much money and time have been spent by companies crafting, redrafting, and editing their mission statements. They work long and hard on creating these statements and hang them up on their walls. So fancy.

The problem is, when you go to any employee (okay, except maybe the ones on the mission statement committee)—or even more important, when you go to customers—and ask them if they know your mission statement, they won't. You will end up with tons of different answers—more than to any other question you could ask about a company.

That's because your mission statement, no matter how nicely it sits on your desk, actually doesn't matter at all. Your mission statement is your actions, and each person who comes in contact with your brand can have a different experience. The statement you make to the world about your goals and what you truly value as a business is not found on a piece of paper. It's found in what you do.

When your wall says that "customers are number one" and yet you make them jump through hoops every time they want to return something, ask a question, or reach a customer service agent, then they are not number one to you. Efficiency, overhead, and not hiring enough customer service representatives are your number one concerns.

It is simply not good enough to spend more energy deciding what our mission statements are than we do listening to our customers. It's not good enough to talk about what our brand is once a year, when we have our yearly business retreat at an overpriced destination. Our mission statements are being written every single day by our customers. Our values are being dictated by the actions of our employees—every day and with every interaction people have with our brand, company, product, or service.

If you want to be UnAwesome, consider these companies as examples, follow their lead, and we'll see you in the next book.[1]

---

[1] Seriously, if you really fark up, shoot me an e-mail and we'll fit you in. This guy needs content. unawesome@un-marketing.com.

Customers Don't See Silos

Being great in social media needs to carry through the resolution chain.

HAVE YOU EVER WAITED in line at a store to return something? Always seems to happen to me on the busiest shopping days, like Black Friday or Boxing Day. And then, once you've waited a very long time, trying to be patient, you get up to the front of the line and somebody tells you, "This isn't the right line."

You have to go line up somewhere else, starting the process all over and giving up even more of your time, effort, and energy. And the whole time you're thinking, "Hey, I'm the customer here. This shouldn't be so hard." If you're returning something, you may already have a negative issue with the store. Or maybe you just want to exchange what you have and turn around and spend even more money. Either way, you don't want to spend more time in another line. I know I never do.

This is what a lot of companies are doing online in social media. Time and time again, I see examples of people tweeting or saying something on Facebook to a brand, looking for resolution, just to be

6

told they are in the wrong line. Sometimes the brand replies directly to let them know that this place (Twitter or their Facebook page) is not the right spot for talking about whatever issue they're having. More often, and worse, no one is manning the account at all, and the customers and their issues are simply ignored and left sitting there.

One of the worst things you can do online as a brand is write in your profile, company description, or even hidden in your notes that your page is "not the place for customer service complaints or inquiries." People don't usually read everything about you on your page before commenting. They just won't see it, and that's why it is such a big problem.

We run our businesses through silos. There's human resources, marketing, and public relations, and then there's customer service. We use these to keep us organized and make sure everything gets done. The thing is, customers don't see silos. They see your brand as a whole. And every time they don't get a response or are told that they're waiting in the wrong line, it hurts your brand. If you have a Twitter account, that is your company. Your Facebook wall is your company—it isn't HR or customer service or PR; it's you. We have to realize that this online place needs to be more of a social traffic control tower, automatically putting customers into the right line, versus one that puts up walls and acts as a gatekeeper.

If you open up the social media doors and people start flooding in, be prepared for them to flood in and say anything, not just what you want them to say or ask. Set up something within your organization so that whoever sees comments will automatically assign them to the right department and reply to the customer. Be sure someone is responsible for letting customers know your brand is listening, cares about their feedback, is taking care of whatever issues may have arisen, and has passed it along to the right people. There is nothing wrong with asking a customer to e-mail you or phone you because you need specific or private information that shouldn't be shared online, but make sure you tell them publicly in your reply.

All of these interactions with customers are changing your brand's impression every single day.

Right now, when people are driving down the road, they don't see the separate silos listed with your department names. All they see is you. And we are changing that brand impression with every interaction. Being great in social media needs to carry through the resolution chain.

How to Flip Off Your Customers

It should never take 10 business days to reply to a customer.

A COUPLE OF CLOSE-TO-HOME examples for me when it comes to silos have to do with the connection, or lack thereof, between a company's social presence and offline presence. Last year, while riding judgmentally in the VIA Rail business class cabin, I happened upon a very unpleasant train attendant. I had apparently wronged her in a past life, and her snarky attitude was something I didn't care for. I felt like she was thinking, "If it wasn't for these passengers, working on this train would be so much better."

While racing down the tracks, I tweeted about my impression and the VIA Rail Twitter account tweeted back almost immediately, wanting to help. They provided me with a customer service e-mail address, where I was asked to better explain what had occurred. All the while, the same train attendant was still dishing out the attitude.[1]

---

[1] Talk about real-time customer service!

After sending the e-mail, I immediately got a reply back and thought, "Wow, being a big deal on Twitter rules!" but it turned out to be an autoresponder, thanking me for my e-mail and warning me that it would be about 10 business days before I would hear back from them. Ten. Business. Days. Not even 10 days. They needed to take weekends into account. So it would take about two weeks to reply back to me. I understand managing expectations, but unless you are writing out each e-mail in chalk and running the slate to somebody up a mountain, it should never take 10 business days to reply to a customer. I then decided to phone in my complaint, and let's just say I would have had a better chance running my complaint up said mountain than talking to anybody with a reasonable amount of intelligence or concern.

This is the problem when we get excited about social media but then drop the brand ball in other departments. Being great in social media and only mediocre or terrible in the rest of your customer service channels is a bad move. Every part of the machine needs to be running at the same level. This is why I don't think social media is the immediate answer for many large companies; first they need to fix their existing customer service issues.

It gets even worse when brands outsource social platforms to a powerless PR agency. I have no problem delegating social media to another company that handles your current communications, but when they have no knowledge, say, or influence over anything outside of a press release, they're a virtual talking head—and one that can't say much.

An example of this is what happened online with the now discontinued Flip video camera. The awesome Chris Farias, who is the Yoda of design, unicorn influencer,[2] and partner at Kitestring Creative Branding Studio,[3] the ones who are responsible for unmarketing.com, decided to tweet the Flip video Canada account about an issue with his camera. You should know that Chris and the entire agency staff were huge fans of the product, but they had a problem with an apparent common fault and decided to tweet about it, because Twitter is their preferred method of communication.

---

[2]Seriously, go check him out on Klout.com.
[3]http://www.kitestring.ca.

The Flip account replied and basically told Chris he was in the wrong line, that his question was a customer service issue, and that he would have to call them. Well, I got wind of this and decided to let them know my thoughts, specifically that they were representing the entire company. The least Flip could do was throw Chris a bone and connect him with someone who could help.

Next thing you know, Chris's phone rings and the guy who runs the Flip account is on the other end. You might think he called to apologize and get Chris a new camera, but no. He actually called and reamed him out, asking why Chris was causing trouble. The Flip account manager explained that he provided only PR for Flip and wasn't responsible for their customer service.

Listen to me very carefully, PR people, social media consultants, divas, and gurus: you are not an extension of your clients' brands; you *are* their brands. You are more their brand than most of the people who work at the company, because you represent the company in the public eye. Anybody running a social media account for a brand should have access to answers and resources within the company, or at least a game plan, for when common issues arise. Otherwise, you might as well not have the account at all.

5

Bright Shiny Objects

Squirrel!

PEOPLE ARE ALWAYS ASKING ME what's next in social media and marketing. But the thing is, we suck at it now. We get so excited by the newest website or technology that we lose focus and forget to work on getting better at what we are already doing.[1]

When we're looking at social media, jumping from shiny new site to shiny new site can undo all the effort we've put in so far. In my first book, we spoke about platforming and how it can take time in social media to build traction, become known, and begin to see the benefits of online engagement. If just when we start getting to know people in one place, we yell "Squirrel!" and run along to the newest site, we have just lost any momentum we were building. It's much more effective to pick a manageable amount of places to be present online and grow

---

[1] We have Angelfire and GeoCities sites that still need work...

11

those before adding new platforms. You don't want to spread yourself too thin or jump ship before really getting to know what a platform has to offer.

We're living in an incredible time, where new technologies are created every day. The online world changes so quickly it is almost impossible to keep up. It's my full-time job to stay on top of what's going on in this stuff and I can hardly count the number of new "game changers" I come across every single day. The truth is, the speed at which the online world grows makes focusing on the newest and brightest really dangerous in business; it's just happening too quickly.

Let's think about apps for a bit. The Apple app store has 500,000 apps listed on their site as of this writing. The Android Market has more than 100,000, and about 20,000 apps are currently available for BlackBerry. Top categories are social networking, music and entertainment, mail and messaging, education and employment, weather, sports, maps, news and current events, and travel.

Doesn't get much brighter and shinier than an app!

When we read about the gazillions of apps downloaded Christmas day, it is easy to jump up and decide our businesses need to have an app. Now. However having an app on iTunes is like having a video on YouTube, just being there doesn't guarantee anything. It doesn't get you views or downloads, and you end up in a crowded space full of your competitors, many of which have better apps and videos than you do. Now you and your shiny, must-have new app are at the high school dance, and everyone else is better looking than you.

The top grossing apps in 2011 were mostly freemium games, where the download and play are free and money is made via user micropurchases along the way. These micropurchases include paying a dollar here and there to fancy up your Smurf Village, for example. They make it easy to play and to pay, brilliant really. So brilliant, in fact, that I hate them, mostly because I didn't come up with the idea myself. The average number of downloads per smartphone downloader is 27 according to Nielsen. This sounds like a lot. Good chance users will choose yours, right? Until you realize those were chosen from a pool of hundreds of thousands. . . .

So then, how do we decide what bright and shiny new technologies to devote precious resources to? Here are some points I think we need to take into account.

- **Identify a market need.** How can the new and shiny help your customer in a new way? Does the site or technology offer something your customers have been looking for? For example, if you run a restaurant and your potential customers are using Yelp.com, or whatever is the newest way to find great places to eat these days, this is technology you should be paying attention to. If you own a printing and framing company and your customers have been asking for easier ways to get their images into your hands, a new app that makes that happen for them would be the perfect new technology to focus on.

- **Make it awesome.** As in every part of your marketing and engagement, make it the best it can be. Be creative. Learn how far all this new stuff can take you to bring your vision of awesome to life. If the cutting-edge platform adds no new value but makes everything more complicated, remind me why we are using it again? We are way too quick to do something just because we can; we need to take time to think about whether we should. I know that you may feel all fancy pants if you have 3D videos shot for your accounting business, but that doesn't make it a good way to spend your precious resources. Decide what would be awesome to your customers; remember, it's not about you.

- **Keep the hoops people have to jump through, the rules, and the guidebook as small as possible.** Be clear and simple. Remember, we are trying to make the experience easy for our customers. When you decide to move your spot for sharing company news and information every six months and ask me to go with you, you're going to lose fans along the way. You can't expect your market to sign up to a new site just to hear about your sales and new products. I am really happy about your new app, but if it should come with a *New App For Dummies* guide, I'm out. Simple and easy. Accessible and useful. New doesn't always mean better.

In the end, all of this new and shiny stuff just means more choices, which is one of the greatest things about technology. Whatever you are going to do, do it right, do it well, and do it awesome.

For updates and more stories about UnAwesome bright and shiny technologies, visit www.TheBookOfBusinessUnAwesome.com/ BrightAndShiny.

6

QR Codes

Every time you use a QR code for something and don't think it through, a kitten dies.

AFTER FARMVILLE, I THINK QR CODES WIN the prize for my most ranted about topic when I'm speaking. They are the perfect example of a bright and shiny marketing object. They are so cool of an idea that they are almost impossible to resist, even when they are clearly the wrong choice for some businesses and situations. I mean look at them. The cool shapes. The way we scan them with our phones and something happens automatically. How can we possibly resist them?!

The problem is when a company decides to use them in places without a signal, they end up spending money on nothing. When we put them on billboards along the highway, where no one could ever possibly scan them, all we say about our business is, "Look, we don't understand technology. Wanna buy our stuff, anyway?" Please don't try to be fancy and include a QR code in your e-mails that I open on my phone. The camera that would scan the QR code is on the back of the same phone. Unless I am some sort of Jedi, I can't scan it. QR codes are just links. If you're sending an e-mail, just put the actual link in the message.

Please do not choose to do something in business just because you can.

Businesses that use QR codes in their newspaper ads or on their for sale signs in front of houses (I'm talking to you, real estate agents) need to make sure that whatever site that code takes me to is mobile-friendly. Remember, I'm scanning the code with my phone, and if the site it takes me to is unreadable, all you are doing is showing me that you don't really care whether it works for me or not. You just wanted to use the newest thing in your ads. With our current technology, it is still often much easier to simply type a web address into my phone than scan your code, so there had better be something awesome on the other end of that link.

Every time you use a QR code for something and don't think it through, a kitten dies—a sweet, innocent kitten. Think before you do. There are a lot of statistics out there about how successful QR codes are. According to a recent report from comScore, some 14 million people scanned QR codes in June 2011,[1] mostly from magazines. Although it is true that we are seeing QR codes everywhere, especially in marketing, we need to make sure that there is true value behind using them. Getting your QR code scanned does not necessarily equal success. Was the scan just a hoop you made someone jump through when it would have been easier simply to type in your site address? Did the scan take the person to a mobile-friendly site with great content? How did the person feel about using the code? Did he or she come back to your site, or did you lose the person afterward? Measuring the number of scans is not enough to call QR codes a success.

Now before you get all, "Hey, Scott, I sure see a whole lot of QR codes in this book for someone who hates QR codes," I do not hate QR codes at all. I think they can be a brilliant tool when used properly. All of the codes in this book, made especially for you, my awesome reader, take you to mobile-friendly places. In the digital version of the book, you will hopefully find links instead of QR codes, because really, you don't need a QR code when you're reading from your iPad. Technology is a beautiful thing when we use it right. If you want to read one of my favorite examples of QR codes done right, check out Chapter 16 on the *Awesome* side, "The Only Good Use for QR Codes."

---

[1] http://on.mash.to/QRCodeStats.

Groupon, Social Commerce Psychology, and Too Many Cupcakes

Everything about Groupon, from site design, the social aspect, the ease of purchase, the deep discounts, and the scarcity of the deal are ideal drivers for "social commerce."

EVERYONE I SPEAK TO WANTS to know about Groupon and whether I think they should give it a try. It's really no wonder everyone is asking about it; Forbes named it the "fastest growing company in web history,"[1] and copycat sites, which were unheard of a few years ago, seem to be popping up everywhere.

Groupon is a daily deal site, offering time-limited discounts. As the customer, you pay upfront and receive a coupon, which is then

---

[1] http://onforb.es/GrouponAwesome.

your responsibility to redeem. Traditionally (back in the ancient times when Groupon started, circa 2008 . . .), the offerings were experiences, such as dinners out or spa services, but more and more types of things are showing up for sale. Now products and even medical services (from dental cleanings to full medicals) can be found on the site.[2]

This is how it works: The deals are based on a certain number of people buying in. Once that number is met, the deal becomes available to everyone who purchased it. This encourages people to share the deals, so enough purchases are made to meet the minimum. If the minimum isn't met, the deals are void and no one gets them. So not only do you want to buy, you want other people to buy, too.

Everything about Groupon, from site design, the social aspect, the ease of purchase, the deep discounts, and the scarcity of the deal are ideal drivers for "social commerce," which is defined as the use of social technology in the context of commerce—that is, selling with social media.[3] Groupon has been as successful as it has by perfectly combining all the reasons people make social purchases or use Social Commerce Psychology:[4] social proof, authority, scarcity, like, consistency, and reciprocity. Let's take a closer look at each one and see how Groupon has mastered them.

- **Social proof:** You can share the deals with your friends and know that they want in, too. People you know, like, and trust also want the same spa getaway at half price. Now you know you want it, too! Groupon also offers a $10 thank you for referring a friend to the site.
- **Authority:** The site stands behind the offers. A deeply discounted dentist visit on Ebay would seem a wee bit risky, but on Groupon you feel secure. The "Groupon Promise" on their home page is an image of a pinky swear and these words: "If the experience using your Groupon ever lets you down, we'll make it right or return your purchase. Simple as that."
- **Scarcity:** Deals are time-limited, so you have to act fast. And share fast. If the minimum isn't met, the purchase is lost.

---

[2] http://bit.ly/GrouponMedical.
[3] http://bit.ly/SocialCommerceDefined.
[4] http://bit.ly/SocialCommercePsychology, http://bit.ly/SocialCommerceInfographic.

- **Like:** People buy things they like. Not exactly rocket science. Groupon offers something for everyone. They target their searches based on information you give them. The better they know you, the better they streamline what you see first.
- **Consistency:** They stay in front of their customers so that when they are looking for deals, Groupon is clearly the place to go. They have an app available for every type of smartphone and send out a daily, targeted newsletter based on the user's location and likes.
- **Reciprocity:** There is a lot of focus on local businesses and how you are supporting companies in your area. Lots of space for each company to create a compelling ad and share how they may be giving back to the community.

These should be our goals when thinking about how we present our product or service every day, with or without Groupon. Ask for testimonials from customers and set yourself up as an authority in your field, an expert. Think about scarcity and how it affects people's choices and get feedback from your customers to find out what they like and are looking for. Stay in front of them to ensure they come back to you. Be consistently moving forward and thinking about ways to give back to them, your community, and the world around you.

Groupon is really no different than any other kind of marketing. You are spending a bit, or taking a cut in this case, to get people in the door the first time. Then your product and service need to stand on their own to keep them coming back. Businesses get exposure from offering discounts on the site, but before you run to sign yourself up, you need to decide if you can afford it. Groupon takes 50 percent of the revenue as their fee, but the business offering the deal does not pay any upfront cost to feature their sale.

Here's the thing, though, and the reason Groupon finds a place in our bright and shiny UnAwesome side: when you offer up a huge discount to your business, in the perfect online selling space, the world is going to come. And you need to be ready for them.

When Need a Cake bakery in the UK decided to give Groupon a try, they had no idea just how popular their deal would be.[5] The bakery offered a dozen cupcakes, typically priced at $40, for $10, a 75 percent

---

[5]http://bit.ly/GrouponCupcakes.

discount. Turns out they were popular, like 8,500 dozen cupcakes (they usually sell 100 dozen per month). That's 102,000 cupcakes at a 75 percent discount. Think about that.

They almost went out of business. The owners had to hire extra workers to come in and keep up. No doubt that current customers were less than impressed when they paid their usual $40 for a dozen.

Most companies go in ready to take a loss and hope these customers will remain happy, paying customers going forward. But what happens when the deal seekers buy their next cupcakes? Will they look for another deal, or will they become loyal to you? Daily deal sites attract deal seekers, and you need to decide if this is where you want to be with your business. If you do decide to give Groupon a try, make sure you can manage the sales and keep your current customers happy while you keep up with the new ones.

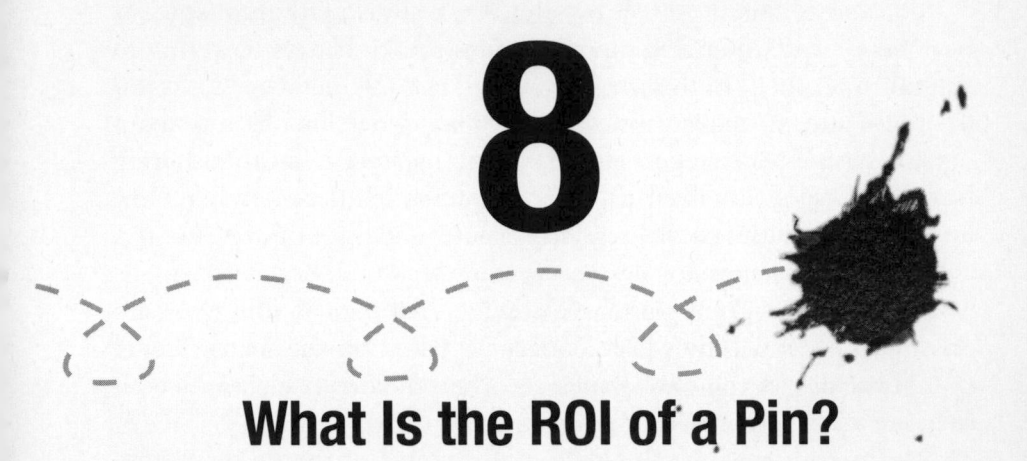

What Is the ROI of a Pin?

Pinterest didn't blow up because of business; it blew up because of passion.

AT THE TIME OF THIS WRITING, the website Pinterest.com is all the rage. If you haven't heard of it, the idea behind it is pretty simple: Pinterest is a virtual pinboard, where people share pictures of things they like online. The majority of the site's users are women.[1]

As I type, Pinterest is the definition of a bright and shiny website, but you can take whatever is the newest, most popular sites right now as you're reading[2] and know that they all find success for one reason: user passion. Sites like Pinterest explode because of their users, who become rabid fans.

---

[1] I am actually pretty sure the site is only women . . . and me. The boards are a plethora of pictures of recipes, amazing hairdos, and Ryan Gosling.

[2] If this was written a few years ago, the site we'd be talking about would be Quora, Gowalla, Google Wave, or Chatroulette. Yeouch.

Of course, bright and shiny sites don't always stay that way. As businesses, we end up breaking these passion-built sites by trying to capitalize on them in the wrong way. I'm not talking about Pinterest finding a way to make money from their users.[3] I'm talking about outside businesses trying to circumvent the system of organic sharing instead of being involved in the community. Pinterest didn't blow up because of business; it blew up because of passion. Awesome is a by-product of passion.

Pushing sales pitches and overcommercializing can kill a website driven by passion. The whole concept is based on the images being shared because of their awesomeness; when users start feeling like all they see are ads, they will stop caring about the content.

Nothing showed me this type of misuse better than a real estate image I saw recently on Pinterest. The picture was of an agent and his partner, standing back to back, arms crossed. They had outsourced the picture to people overseas to like and repin to make it look as popular as possible.[4] This kind of fake awesome makes me crazy. It dilutes the amazing content on the site and makes truly awesome stuff harder to find.

If you want to see a company doing it right, check out the Whole Foods Pinterest page: http://pinterest.com/wholefoods/. They understand how to share their brand within a passionate community. They do more than just pin pictures of their logo and products. They share images they know their customers will love, like those of amazing kitchen remodels. On Pinterest, they make themselves a catalyst for their customers' passion, not just a billboard for ads.

Like all the bright and shiny technologies out there, cool new websites like Pinterest are great, but you don't have to use them. You don't need to be on Pinterest. What you do need to do is realize that your customers may be, and you need to have your content ready to share. Think about the images on your site and how you can make them look as good as possible. Then include sharing buttons on your blog posts and pin buttons to your product pages. If you do decide to have your company on there, please jump in and be a part of the community. And never, ever ask, "What is the ROI of a pin?"

---

[3] They eventually have to make money right? Right?! Or be bought by Facebook for a billion dollars . . . hello Instagram.

[4] I just dry heaved in my mouth just thinking about it.

9

Skippy the Social Scaler

POW, POW, POW!!!

ONE OF THE SOLUTIONS that's offered for managing the overwhelming number of platforms out there is automation, or as I called it social scaling.

These bright and shiny technologies give you the ability to try to be everywhere at once, without ever really being anywhere at all. I cannot tell you enough times that social media isn't about how many places you can be; it's about being amazing where you are.

When I think about social scaling, I picture an infomercial, kind of like this . . .

Introducing Skippy the Social Scaler!

Why actually spend time in social media when you can tell the whole world every crappy part of your life all day, every day and never have to hear their reply!

That's right, Skippy the Social Scaler here, taking the social out of social media since 2011!

You just had a tuna sandwich, tell them POW, POW, POW!!! MYSPACE LINKEDIN TWITTER FACEBOOK GOOGLE+ ALL UPDATED (doin' finger guns)

The world can hear about the crappy details of your life, without ever having to reply back! Don't have 8 seconds to tweet. POW, POW!!

You can be in only one place at a time. That's just a fact. You can use technology to keep up with a lot of stuff at once, you can create evergreen ways to stay in front of your audience, but in the end, you and your attention are not scalable.

The new and shiny technologies that make you think you can scale your online relationships are lying to you. If you don't have the 30 seconds it takes to write a proper Facebook update, rather than link your tweet full of hashtags using the newest social scaling technology, you are trying to be in too many places. Stop it. If your tweets are all cut off halfway through with a Facebook post link, you aren't really tweeting. And people know it. You come off as someone who really doesn't think his or her audience is worth the time for a proper message. When I follow you on one site and your posts all take me to another, eventually I will stop clicking.

The one caveat is when your brand is of the level that it gets mentioned on so many platforms at once that you couldn't keep up. In this case you need to employ a listening tool. Optimizing your listening is fine. Using a tool such as Radian6 or Vocus can really help steer you through the online noise and help you prioritize which platforms to focus time on. Then use that extra time to reply, for real, and be there for the conversation.

10

Mobile Madness

If I can't consume, buy, or share your content, what exactly is the point of having it?

IN THE LAST FEW CHAPTERS, we've been talking about all things bright and shiny in business, and I've been telling you to treat them with caution. Generally, when new technologies come along, I want you to check them thoroughly before you leap. Remember, being awesome online is about being great where you are, not jumping around and trying to be everywhere.

This topic, however, is different. Mobile technology is not something you can ignore, or even stand back and wait around for. Mobile is here, and it needs to be a critical part of your business. A ton of studies have been conducted about the growth of mobile use. More than any other technology out there, mobile is the growth leader.[1] In 2011, for

---

[1]http://heidicohen.com/mobile-marketing-must-have-facts/.

the first time, smartphone and tablet shipments exceeded desktop and notebook shipments.[2]

Mobile is important for all aspects of our business, from marketing to customer service and sales. If you choose to use social media for any, or all, of these parts of business, the growth in access to social media from phones is amazing. More than 72 million Americans accessed social networking sites or blogs via their mobile devices in August 2011, a figure that represents a 37 percent jump from the same time last year, according to data compiled by comScore.[3] Depending on which study you look at, anywhere between now and 2014, the Internet is or will be accessed on more frequently from mobile platforms than from computers.

Please understand, having your website come up on my phone does not mean you are successful at mobile. It's not so much that businesses are ignoring the technology of mobile; it's just that they are failing miserably at being there properly. When thinking about this chapter and just how important mobile is, I decided to bring in my wonderful, equally angry and sarcastic friend Sara Santiago from Roll Mobile to set you all straight.

Just plug in UnMarketing.com on your phone and check out her handiwork. Sara knows a thing or two about mobile.

Crappy Mobile Web Experience (AKA How to Lose a Customer in 10 Seconds)

Recently, I read an article quoting a "mobile expert" as saying that brands don't need a mobile website, rather a few well-designed apps. This was a *recent* article. (For those of you that know me well, I was well past the eye twitch and moving quickly toward head explosion.) When I read things like this, my staff can hear the random bursts of obscenities and loud sighs of "Idiots!" coming from the corner office. They've learned to give me a good half hour or so to calm down.

---

[2] http://blog.flurry.com/bid/63907/Mobile-Apps-Put-the-Web-in-Their-Rear-view
-Mirror.
[3] http://mashable.com/2011/10/20/mobile-social-media-stats/.

Okay, in all seriousness. I give these experts no mercy because they are out there pumping themselves up as "experts" and spreading useless or nonsensical "expert insight" into mobile. I had generally given less informed or ill-informed brands a bit of leeway due to lack of education and guidance from their digital representation. Today, however, it's time for all brands, marketers, large advertisers, and agencies to step up their game in mobile. Make all the excuses you want for not having a mobile website. Your competition will thank you.

Here is an example of something that makes me twitchy:

79% of large advertisers do not have a mobile optimized website.

—Google, May 2011

(Pauses to regain composure. Looks something like Figure 10.1.)

Figure 10.1   The Crappy Mobile Website Facepalm

Source: © Sara Santiago, June 2011. Used with permission.

Seventy-nine percent. Seventy. Nine. When we know that mobile users overwhelmingly prefer the mobile web for product

(*continued*)

(*continued*)

reviews (79%), video (58%), researching prices (81%), and looking for businesses and restaurants, maps, and store locations (64%). Think about it. You want to look up that new restaurant, shopping center, movie review, concert venue, or [insert awesome thing here]. Where do you go? I'd be willing to bet a lot of you open the browser on your phone and start with your search engine of choice. In short, you Google it.

Here's a recent example of how to lose a customer by not thinking about what the user wants in a mobile experience. This is a standard retail purchase and could play out differently for different types of business, but you're all really wicked-smart, and you'll get the gist.

The following story is based on actual events. Some of the names have been changed.

SARA: Googles "Awesome Thing" in mobile browser; selects AwesomeStore.com.

AWESOMESTORE.COM: Renders mobile-formatted splash page that reads "Download our super cool app in your app store by clicking this link. OR click this other link to go to our website."

SARA: Not wanting to leave this site to open app store, download native app, create user login, etc., clicks link to website.

AWESOMESTORE.COM: Loads desktop-formatted website.

SARA: "Okay. You know I'm on a phone, so after you detect my device, you provide me an option to download your app. I choose not to, and STILL KNOWING I'M ON A MOBILE PHONE, you render a desktop-formatted site." (Eyeball begins to twitch.) WTF?!

AWESOMESTORE.COM: Still renders a desktop-formatted site, no matter how much Sara blinks and curses.

SARA: Returns to original Google search and selects Other-AwesomeStore.com (competitor of AwesomeStore).

OTHERAWESOMESTORE.COM: Mobile-formatted site loads. (Double rainbow!)

SARA: Reads product info and reviews of "Awesome Thing" she's looking for. It really *is* awesome. She clicks to purchase. (Can choose from several payment methods.) Chooses to pay with PayPal.

OTHERAWESOMESTORE.COM: E-mails receipt and shipping confirmation to Sara's phone.

SARA: Immediately tells Twitter that "Awesome Thing" is on its way and thanks OtherAwesomeStore.com for such a fast, intuitive, mobile website. All is right in Sara's world. Ministroke avoided . . . this time.

Seriously folks. If you haven't done anything to address the ever growing amount of smartphone (and more sophisticated feature phone) usage (and mobile search!), start now. Make sure that your website is optimized for mobile devices. Keep the following in mind:

- Respect the UX, more than ever, user experience is key. Users are becoming more savvy and will tolerate less crap. Poor user experience could cost you a customer very quickly. Some brands are setting the bar high, the user is becoming accustomed to easy, intuitive, user experience while taking advantage of the new technologies the mobile devices offer. Get your thinking caps on. (These ain't yer mama's WAP sites, homies.)
- Prioritize content with mobile user in mind, and always provide the option to access the traditional site in case the user needs to hunt for something specific and not available on the mobile site. (Use mobile detection and redirection to load mobile initially, but allow for self selection of desktop content.)

(continued)

(*continued*)
- Users have the *NEED* for SPEED, and they hold grudges. Google recently reported that 61% of mobile users won't return to a site that they couldn't access quickly (had trouble or delay loading) from this mobile device.
- Beware of "Shiny New Object" syndrome. Just because it's fancy, new, and exciting doesn't mean it's a good fit for your mobile Web experience. Much of the time, less is more.

AWESOME UX—FAST, INTUITIVE, CONVENIENT, LOCATION-BASED, mPAYMENT = WINNING.

So there you have it, folks. You've spent a lot of time creating successful Web experiences and, in some cases, e-commerce experiences for your customers. Mobile users are ready. They'll be looking for you on their mobile devices. What will they find?

Source: Sara Santiago, "Crappy Mobile Web Experience..." © Sara Santiago, June 2001. http://bit.ly/SaraIsAwesome.

See what I mean about Sara? Awesome, right?!

I remember the first time I met Sara. She was speaking at the same event I was, and everything she said made me feel like I was in the choir of the greatest sarcasm church of all time. I may have even said "Hallelujah" out loud once or twice.

You need to understand this one basic idea about mobile and why it can't be ignored. If I spend more and more of my time accessing the Internet from my phone but I can't access your content effectively when I reach your site, this means I can't consume it. If I can't consume it, I can't buy it or share it. And, if I can't consume, buy, or share your content, what exactly is the point of having it there?

You don't need an app. You don't need to use QR codes. You need to change your mind-set first. Start by cleaning your site and making it mobile-friendly; then, and only then, look at other new technologies. Until then, don't you even mention the newest fancy bell or whistle out there, or Sara and I are going to show up at your door.

11

Data Is Dangerous

Data without insights is just ignorance.

WE SEE DATA POINTS EVERYWHERE in business, most of the time up on screens from speakers like me who are trying to prove that what we're saying is right. In reality, data is dangerous. In fact, 67 percent of all data is made up.[1]

To explain why it can be harmful, I've asked my data diva, and one of the smartest guys I know, Tom Webster, who is the vice president of strategy at Edison Research, to share his thoughts on this important point.

---

[1]You see what I did there?

Clicks, Cakes, and the Limits of Social Media "Science"

There is an apocryphal story in the annals of market research that I particularly love about *cake mix* (*apocryphal*, by the way, is Greek for "a pile of crap," so this probably isn't true—but I'll tell the story anyway).

The story goes that back in the 50's, Betty Crocker had developed its first completely one-box cake mix—just add water and bake. After some initial buzz, sales began to disappoint, so the Betty Crocker executives did a series of focus groups to suss out the problem.

Imagine tackling this problem today, using social media monitoring, or tracking clickstream behavior. Betty Crocker might observe fewer clicks to their recipe page, or perhaps fewer positive mentions. Coupon activity from register scans might decline. Positive sentiment for Duncan Hines might increase. We might learn that the best time to tweet about cakes is 10:00 AM on a Sunday. Maybe we'd record an increase in the number of tweets about the poor quality of Betty Crocker's mix.

We could take all of this online behavior—all of these tweets and clicks—and determine a few things. Some of our conclusions would be correct, while others would be off the mark. Mining this information is crucial to the lifeblood of the organization—don't get me wrong. But bits and bytes will only ever tell you the *what*. They rarely give you the straight story on the *why*.

One thing I've learned in about 20 years of doing qualitative research—people are not as expressive about products and services as we'd like them to be. Often, we cannot clearly articulate what makes us uncomfortable, or dissatisfied, with a given product, so we fall back on the easy answers. "It doesn't taste right." "It costs too much." "I don't have enough time." These are the first things I hear in any focus group, before Stockholm syndrome really sets in. This is when the experienced qualitative researcher reaches into their bag of tricks and helps the respondents along—and uncovers the real reasons behind these perceptions of quality, value, and importance. These data, of

course, are anecdotal until you can test these assumptions, and social media is providing us with more and more tools to do just that. But social media often gives us the easy answers—not the true answers.

Back to Betty Crocker. Unable to mine Twitter, our 1950s executives did a series of focus groups with housewives that had tried, and ultimately rejected, their cake mix. Much to their surprise, they realized that these ladies thought the cakes tasted just fine and were pretty good values. Instead, the insight they developed over time was that the cake mixes were a little *too* easy. In postwar America, as their husbands worked long days, these stay-at-home moms were a little embarrassed about the fact that all they had to do to have a delicious cake on the table for their men to enjoy after work was just add water and stir. In short, they felt guilty.

This is why you now have to add an egg, or perhaps a little oil, to a cake mix. Certainly these ingredients could be incorporated into the package—we do have a little history of food science in this country. But adding these one or two ingredients made it feel like *baking* again, and not just assembling. These women didn't just want cakes—they wanted to *feel good*.

The numbers only give you half the story—and I say this as someone who makes his living telling the stories of numbers. The operative word there, of course, is *story*. It's easy to be seduced by social media data, especially by those who loudly proclaim that they have the numbers on their side. Numbers aren't on anyone's side. I've had a lifelong battle with them, trust me. Adding insights to data is more than just putting flesh on the bones of an otherwise solid skeleton. Often, you don't know what you think you know merely by dredging tweets.

No, data without insights is just *ignorance*.

Source: Tom Webster, "Clicks, Cakes, and the Limits of Social Media 'Science.'" www.brandsavant.com. Used with permission.

To see more of Tom's brilliance, check him out at BrandSavant.com, and if you ever see him in person, ask him to do his Sean Connery impression.

12
Toyota Punk'd

I don't know if the moral of this story is data is dangerous, or morons are dangerous.

HERE IS A PRESENT-DAY example of how, as Tom Webster from the previous chapter, said, "data without insights is just ignorance," and it demonstrates the results of a campaign based too highly on numbers and not enough on good sense.

When Amber Duick received a series of threatening e-mails from a strange man, she did what any of us would do: she freaked out. Over a few days, a man who knew her address sent her e-mails telling her he was on the run from the police and heading to her house. These e-mails were all part of a Toyota ad campaign for the Matrix, developed based on research that showed their target market, 20-something-year-old males, love pranking their friends.

A friend of Amber's signed her up to be pranked at www .YourOtherYou.com. She received a first e-mail, asking for permission to participate in some kind of interactive activity, thought it

sounded like fun, and went on with her day, never expecting what was coming. The idea was that she would end up on the Toyota site and be told it was a trick, but Amber was terrified by the e-mails, long before finding out it was a prank.

She sued Toyota and others associated with the campaign for $10 million for emotional distress, misrepresentation, and unlawful trade practices.[1]

Do 20-something males like pranking their friends? Most likely. Are most Toyota Matrixes purchased by 20-somethings? Sounds like it. Does that mean pranking the unassuming public is a good marketing campaign? Absolutely not. I would have to say that cyber-stalking is the last thing anyone wants their brand associated with.

I don't even know where to begin with this. I can picture all the wannabe Ashton Kutchers, sitting around a boardroom table with their client's budget, congratulating each other on how awesome this was going to be. It is not enough to take the basic conclusions of what 20-something males may or may not like and use that, without the addition of common sense, to plan a campaign. Clearly, other people would come into contact with the prank, and frightening strangers cannot be the basis of a marketing plan.

I don't know if the moral of this story is data is dangerous, or morons are dangerous. But the combination will get you sued.

---

[1] http://www.wired.com/threatlevel/2011/09/toyota-punkd/.

13

Kids Don't Play in Crappy Playgrounds

Numbers give you only half the story.

I WAS DOING A WEBINAR for the apartment management industry when I realized data can be dangerous. A person listening took issue with my suggestion that Facebook was a great place to create a virtual community for people living within their properties. She quoted a statistic about how unsuccessful industry Facebook pages had been in the past. She had taken the data and come to the conclusion that focusing on Facebook was entirely a waste of time for apartment managers.

This assumption could not be more wrong. Let me explain why.

Let's say 20 properties in her city all had playgrounds on their properties. The playgrounds included one rock, a broken bottle, and a dead bird. If you surveyed those apartment dwellers, data would show that nobody used the playgrounds. Ever. We could take that information and conclude, as the woman had, that there was no reason

to add a playground to your new apartment complex. After all, no one would be using it anyway.

The reality is, it's not that apartment complexes don't need playgrounds. The conclusion should be that kids don't play in crappy playgrounds, rather than make it as simple as taking the data and drawing a conclusion about playgrounds, or Facebook pages, in general. We need to look at the quality of these and the why behind lack of use.

Nobody engages on a crappy Facebook page if all your apartment page shows is new ads. If we take that online space and create community, with dialog and resources, people will come. Facebook is not an answer; it's a tool. We need to use it properly to facilitate community. It won't just happen because "we have a Facebook page."

It is actually a smaller example of a bigger problem. Using a benchmark in general in social media isn't smart. Saying Facebook doesn't work or Twitter does work makes no sense. These are all tools, and just like a hammer doesn't build a house, a social media platform doesn't make a successful business. When used properly, your community will see that you are actually listening and give a damn. They will come, they will stay, and they will even play.

We cannot make business decisions based on numbers alone. People are not numbers, and they cannot be expected to act the same way numbers do. As Tom Webster said in an earlier chapter, "numbers give you only half the story," a valuable half, but not the whole. Beware of what "social meida scientists" tell you.

The UnSilent Minority

Most of the world goes quietly about their business and will speak up or out about an experience only when it is really extreme.

ONE OF THE OTHER ISSUES in focusing on statistics, especially those collected from reports or feedback, is that most of the time the majority of people are quiet. In my first book, I wrote a chapter titled "Don't Bank on the Bold" and spoke about how giving too much weight to the loudest of our critics, or supporters for that matter, is not always a wise decision.

Tom Webster, who shared his writing in an earlier chapter, also speaks about this in his blog post titled "What Your Brand Needs to Know about the Social Media Caucus."[1] He talks about elections and how the sentiments of online voices are usually so far off from what actually ends up happening in an election. According to Tom,

---

[1] http://bit.ly/BrandSavant.

he has never seen a *"repeatable* correlation between social media mentions/sentiment and the actual vote."

He goes on to say that, "To date I have not been presented with a replicable model which shows, candidate for candidate, that the number of people tweeting about a politician has anything to do with the number of people in Cedar Falls, Iowa, who actually got in a car, drove to a high school gymnasium, and raised their hand."

He suggests we take this into consideration for our business and consider what this means for mentions of our brands online and people actually choosing to act and buy something from us.

Most of the world goes quietly about their business and will speak up or out about an experience only when it is really extreme. The great power of social media as a listening tool is how we can harness the passive conversations our market is having online. We don't need to wait for the voices of the bold, or as I call them, the UnSilent Minority.

The thing is, if we open up our listening to passive conversations, listen to a larger group, and listen over time, we can see a picture of our brand take shape.

15

Respect the Inbox

Newsletter apathy is really the biggest problem we face in trying to stay in front of our market.

THERE ARE HUNDREDS, if not thousands, of studies out there talking about how frequently we should e-mail our customers, our target market, and even one another.

Now frankly, I don't really care what the studies say. It's dangerous to read studies, review the data, and think, "That worked for them, so that is a great business practice." I read a study recently that talked about how you can e-mail your customer list, your target list, or your lead list daily and you don't lose that many subscribers, compared with sending your newsletter out only once a week.

A threshold of complete annoyance to the point of people walking out the door and quitting should *not* be one we're aiming for. We should *not* aim for that frequency of newsletter distribution that falls at just being tolerated. Our goal should be for our customer base to open

our newsletter—to anticipate it, to look forward to it. We want them to treat it as something that they want to read—not just tolerate.

It isn't enough to focus only on staying out of the spam folder. I want to see a study about how many people receive but still never see newsletters. They may not unsubscribe, but they have simply stopped caring. Newsletter apathy is the biggest problem we face in trying to stay in front of our market.

E-mail marketing is still an extremely effective tool in this day and age of social media sexiness, but only if done right. It isn't enough to simply look at unsubscribe numbers. If the bar with which you measure success is set as low as the point where people actively kick you out of their inbox, you are setting your standards too low. It's like saying door-to-door sales are successful because none of the people who've answered your knocks this week tried to stab you. Not getting stabbed should not be a measure of success. We can do better than that.

Your entire goal of sending a newsletter to your audience is to have them open it, react to it, and spread it. Getting past the filters and not receiving unsubscribe requests is not enough. When was the last time someone saw your newsletter and loved it so much he or she had to share it? This should be the level of awesome we are aiming for.

Some business experts will tell you that it's a great idea to send a birthday message out to your customer list when customers have added their birthdays to their profiles. I think a little "Happy Birthday" is always a great thing, but that does not make it an invitation to sell them something. A discount on your products, which still means the customer has to give you money, isn't a birthday present. The greatest birthday e-mail I got from a brand this year was from Cirque du Soleil. They sent me a happy birthday wish, and that was it. Not 10 percent off, which means, "We want you to spend 90 percent of our asking price on your birthday. Congratulations!" They simply said happy birthday, and that was it. And it was actually a great reverse mind ninja move that made me want to go check out their site and see their upcoming shows. All because they didn't try to sell me.

When I think about companies and respecting the inbox, two personal examples come to mind. Both examples are of great gift companies I was introduced to, and I was really happy with the quality of their products: FTD.com and HarryAndDavid.com. I had made purchases with both companies and signed up for their newsletters.

The thing is, I didn't stay signed up for long because they dropped the brand ball when it came to marketing.

Customer lists do not fall under the rules of the CAN-SPAM[1] Act of 2003, which governs e-mail marketing, but businesses should not interpret this as license to piss off the people on their lists. Once I had signed up for their newsletters, both companies started e-mailing me incessantly, sometimes even daily about their special offers. I had not forgotten, between newsletters, that FTD sells flowers. I had not forgotten, since the e-mail the day before, that Harry and David sell great pear baskets and other gifts.

Being reminded too often, in all caps fashion, really irritated me. They didn't respect the space I had given them in my inbox, and I ultimately unsubscribed. I, a happy customer, who had willingly given my e-mail and contact information, opted out of the newsletters.

I know what the stats say. Most of them say to keep e-mailing. The thing is, you do piss people off and pissed off people will unsubscribe. You take happy customers and irritate them to the point where they remove themselves from your e-mail database. You lose the opportunity to share promotions and information with them, all because of the ridiculous and excessive frequency with which you've been sending out newsletters. The lack of respect, for my time and for my inbox, means that I don't want to be in touch anymore. You had gotten all the way over that hurdle of having me become a customer to the point where I am done. And that's not where we want to go.

One of the most disturbing practices in business newsletters is when you meet someone at a networking event and exchange cards, mostly because the other person just handed you one and, feeling obligated, you gave him or her one in reciprocation. Then, after handing over the card, you realize the next week that person signed you up for his or her newsletter. People who do this are showing a huge lack of respect, not only for my inbox, but also for the connection we just made.

Me handing you my business card is not a newsletter opt in. I am not dying to know what you're up to in a mass, generically sent way; the point of a business card exchange is to extend the one-to-one conversation. And if you'd like to ask me if I want to join your

---

[1] http://en.wikipedia.org/wiki/CAN-SPAM_Act_of_2003.

newsletter in an e-mail, that's different. But automatically signing me up is a great way to hurt the relationship you just began to create.

Newsletters are a great way to stay in front of our market and position ourselves as experts, but only when done with respect. Share great content and set the expectation of how often you will be in touch before the person signs up, so they know what to expect. When you respect your list, they will open your newsletter, they will share, and they will buy from you.

16

Lies Internet Marketers Tell

Making money is not a business; it's the result of good business.

MY MARKETING ROOTS were planted early on in Internet marketing circles.[1] The Make Money Online world makes telemarketers look like saints. It's basically just people making money by telling people how to make money by selling them programs about how to make money.

When we talk about e-mail, and not respecting the inbox, Internet marketers' practices are the worst of all. Here are some of the worst of the worst—lies Internet marketers tell.

They teach techniques such as using misleading subject lines, for example, by encouraging people to put "Re:" at the start to make it look as though they are replying to you about something when in reality it's just a promotion for their new product.

They actually shouldn't even use the term *newsletter* for what they send. A while ago, I signed up for dozens of Internet marketing

---

[1] Which is why I still feel kinda dirty.

"newsletters" to actually see which ones provided good content versus sales pitches. The answer was zero. Not one of them provided any kind of content unconditionally. Every lesson, every story, and every teaching led to a new product of theirs or their friends. The craziest thing about it is that they'd use these techniques to sell you a program to teach you how to use the exact same techniques they just used on you. Making money is not a business; it's the result of good business. You can use the Internet to greatly help your business, but the Internet should not be the business.

- **They use false scarcity.** I'm pretty sure an e-product can't actually sell out. Scarcity is created for both time to purchase (this week only!) and number available (only 100 e-books available!).

  They will put a limit on the number of people who can buy a digital product just to make you think it could run out. When the cutoff number for purchases is reached, many marketers will then e-mail people on their lists again with the exciting news: after sorting through orders, they've found a few duplicates, or have given a refund or two, and can now offer you an amazing, entirely unexpected opportunity to purchase![2]

- **They delay the delivery of certain modules of content.** Internet marketers do this so that the buyer doesn't receive the modules until more than 30 days after the date of original purchase. Most credit card companies give you 30 days to decide if you are satisfied with your purchase. If you're not, you can get a refund. Delaying delivery until this period has passed makes the marketers immune to refunds.

- **They suck you into live events.** Tickets to events are either given away as part of purchase or sold at a discounted price to customers just to fill the seats. The issue I have is that, more often than not, these events are just long, glorified sales pitches. Speakers are brought in on their own dime and forced to sell from the stage. The organizer takes half of what the speakers earn from the sales, and the audience is once again tricked into paying for any and all content.

---

[2] I really need a sarcasm font.

Sadly, when we fast-forward six months down the road, the product you spent your hard-earned money on is now being given away for free as an added bonus to their latest program—just part of the newest pitch from them or a friend.

- **They tell you the demand was so great that the servers crashed.** The common scenario is that they launch a new product and then blast a second e-mail out to everyone on their list, claiming that their product was so popular it crashed their server. They want to make sure you still get a chance to give them your money! So let me get this straight: you are trying to tell your audience that you are a professional millionaire on the Internet, yet your site lives on a server that can't handle the 36 orders that came in on one day? I think its time to upgrade your AOL account.

- **They will regularly "forget" to declare their affiliate relationship with other products, either on Twitter, on blogs, or in e-mail.** This practice takes advantage of readers' trust and violates Federal Trade Commission (FTC) rules.

  FTC rules state that you must disclose any commercial relationship to any product that you mention anywhere online (via tweet, blog, e-mail, etc.). These were recent updates to the law that were necessary because of the predominance of online recommendations. It's not enough to have a blanket statement somewhere on your site that discloses that you may have an affiliate relationship with some brands. The disclosure has to be with the recommendation, which causes a slippery slope when it comes to things like tweets where you're limited in characters. I'm many things; none of which are a lawyer. So please consult with one if you have real questions about this.

  Some people use the hashtags #sponsor or #affiliate in a tweet; I usually use the word *client*, if it's necessary. In reality, it shouldn't take the FTC to make us be transparent in business. If the general public wouldn't obviously know that a financial relationship exists, we need to make them aware.

- **They make it time-consuming to opt out.** *Opt out* is not Latin for "more"! If it takes 30 seconds to sign up for a newsletter, that is exactly how long it should take to unsubscribe. Why piss people off when they're walking out the door?

One of the faults of bigger brands, outside of Internet marketing circles, is their e-mail policy. I recently unsubscribed from a large brand e-mail list just to be told that it would take up to 10 days to remove me. Wait . . . what? How are they removing the e-mail address? Is it through a Post-it Note system, where somebody has to run back to a room and manually pull out a piece of paper? Amazingly, when I signed up for the list, I was instantly added. I know they say 10 days because that's what's in the CAN-SPAM Act, but come on. Instantly on should mean instantly off. Even when I was running a list manually back in the day, through Outlook, I could search an e-mail address and remove it in a few seconds. My unsubscribing from your list does not mean I hate your brand, but feeding me lines like this, could.

- **They inundate you with e-mails.** I understand trying to find out the optimal time to e-mail everyone on your list and thinking about how frequently you should reach out for the best results, but being skeezy to get a higher open rate on e-mails simply isn't worth it.

  Frequency can be a matter of conditioning. If I sign up for a daily deal site like Groupon, I expect a daily e-mail. But if I'm a new customer who just bought something online from you, that doesn't mean that I'm hoping to buy something every day from now on. At the very least, condition the expectations of subscribers by telling them when they sign up how frequently they will be receiving e-mails. I can't count the number of brands that I am a customer of that inundated me with e-mails after I signed on to the point that I unsubscribed—they lost a customer who was initially willing to listen. This month alone I have unsubscribed to four brand e-mails after becoming a customer. As we discussed earlier, the CAN-SPAM Act doesn't apply to customer lists, but that's not a reason to abuse your readers.

Are there legitimate products out there? Of course. There are some really smart products that have to do with search engine optimization (SEO) and video and sales techniques. But in a sea of unethical floaters, it's very rare to find the good ones.

Even though Internet and e-mail marketing have formed many of the worst business practices, there are ways for it to be great for your

business. Every time somebody signs up for a newsletter, that person is waving a hand in the air to say he or she wants to learn from you or likes your brand. One of the simplest ways to start the relationship off right is to start a conversation with them (something I mentioned in my first book). I ask every subscriber to the UnMarketing newsletter what line of business he or she is in, and that question always starts a conversation. Obviously, if you're a bigger brand, this technique may not be scalable, but you could invite new subscribers to a welcome post on your brand's Facebook page to have a conversation with other brand enthusiasts.

This is one of those windows I'm talking about where we have an opportunity to be awesome, even on the smallest digital scale. When so many e-mail lists are battered and bruised, it is easy to stand out and be great. Give it a try.

Warm Spam

Be nice, be helpful, and don't FUCC people, and social media can be the greatest thing in the world.

BACK IN THE OLD DAYS of the Internet and e-mail, it was a happy place (we'll call this time period BS: "before spam"). In the BS years, the Internet was pure information and e-mail was a way to communicate useful information and have a conversation with someone. Every time an e-mail came in, it was like a little butterfly of excitement flew into your computer, and you knew it contained an ingredient of awesome. Then something changed. E-mail started getting UnAwesome.

Cold callers, cold knockers (those who went door to door), and car smackers (those who placed flyers on cars' windshields), realizing that their methods of sales assault worked less and less, had found a place where they barely had to lift a finger to push their useless wares on the public. "Now we can e-mail our crap!" and proceeded to group high-five (which is now evolved to awkward fist-bumping).

The owners of the inboxes became angry and classified anything they didn't ask for as unsolicited commercial e-mail (UCE)—or SPAM

for short. Laws were passed, Internet service providers (ISPs) set up block lists, and the word was spread: "People don't like spam. Stop it."

If you are accused of being a spammer, it's the biggest shame there is in business.

Now there is a bigger problem: warm spam or social spam. Or as I like to refer to it, friendly unsolicited commercial contact (FUCC). It's the practice of spamming your social media contacts, and it needs to stop.

Think about it: someone finally accepts you as a contact on LinkedIn, follows you on Twitter, or friends you on Facebook, and you apparently believe that's Yiddish for "SELL, SELL, SELL!"

It's actually worse than old-school spam. We can delete or block messages from faceless spammers and think evil thoughts about them, but with social spam, you sometimes know the person in real life, so removing or blocking the person can cause more awkwardness than seeing Uncle Louis at Christmas dinner after he poked you on Facebook.

Some common warm spam techniques include:

- **Sending invites to real events:** These are invitations to events that someone sends to his or her entire friend list, regardless of geographic/demographic makeup.
- **Sending invites to fake events:** These are invitations to events that are actually nonevents. For example, the invite could be for a "website launch party" or "Vote for me because my self-esteem is based on artificial online popularity campaigns." It's not even the issue of the "event" itself, but the relentless inviting and messaging people who haven't RSVP'd for an event that doesn't exist tends to make people stabby.
- **Sending LinkedIn e-mails that show everyone's e-mail address:** Nothing like someone e-mailing everyone about his or her upcoming paralegal training seminar through LinkedIn, which exposes our private e-mail addresses to one another! Yes, this just happened.
- **Tagging:** Mostly on Facebook, but now creeping into Google+, this refers to the practice of tagging someone in a pic or post for the sole purpose of making that person view it or read it and have it appear on his or her timeline.
- **Using auto-DM:** Tweeting someone about your Facebook fan page as soon as that person follows you on Twitter is like shaking

someone's hand at a networking event and then asking if he or she wants to go to another event down the street.

- **Publicly shaming others:** Asking someone to support a cause publicly by adding their Twitter name is like asking someone to support your charity at an event with other people standing around. Ask privately or post a general support message. Don't shame people.
- **Requesting fans for your Facebook page:** Inviting people to "fan" your business by sending a request hurts my brain. Add it to your blog, put it in the signature in your e-mail, but going out and picking people to be fans is just awkward.
- **Managing farms run by MafiaVille:** I know you want more coins, land, bullets, or whatever they're offering you to invite "your friends" to play a game of FarmVille/Mafia Wars/The Sims, but stop it. While you're tending to your farm, we talk about you behind your virtual back.[1]

When someone subscribes to your list, or follows your company, that does not mean that they have given you permission to send out any and all e-mails. You need to look at what I call the "condition of permission." If they follow your clearance site Twitter account, where you tweet sales, then this is the condition they've signed up for. However, if they sign up for your monthly newsletter, for updates on tips for small business, you can't take that list and blast sales at them. If you do, you've broken the permission condition, one of the worst types of warm spam.

Relax your pitchforks, "real" businesspeople; I'm not saying never sell. I'm not even suggesting social media is a sacred ground never to be sold on. It's the method. Your wall on Facebook is yours; do as you please. You want to tweet about your upcoming teleclass? Knock yourself out. You lease that space. However, as soon as you add my @UnMarketing to the tweet or tag someone on a page, well, now you've FUCC'ed it—especially if that action also generates an e-mail to that person, because now you've spammed my e-mail with the notification. Double FUCC'ed.

---

[1] Thanks to Amanda Wood for the reminder on this one!

Your wall, your profile—your real estate. Post as many promos as you want. But you'll soon realize that nobody is sharing, liking, clicking, or retweeting them. Now, a logical person would realize, "Hey, maybe people aren't engaging with my ads because they don't really like ads in a social setting." But sadly, most react by thinking, "People aren't clicking because they missed it! I'll just post this on their page, too!"

Nobody has joined a social media site to get sold to, but people do actually buy from people they know, like, and trust—things that are created by being social with others. See that equation. Be nice, be helpful, and don't FUCC people, and social media can be the greatest thing in the world.

18

Social Is Human

If you want to increase your bottom line, improve your front line.

BACK IN THE DAY (easy now...it's not that long ago), I used to be in HR, and I don't think I would be able to handle the madness that happens today with employees when it comes to social media.

As far as I'm concerned, HR is the most crucial component of a company. If you don't hire the right people, nothing that marketing or sales can do for you will matter. The old "warm body" syndrome, where hiring would simply mean filling in lower-paid positions in your company with anyone who came along, is really asking for trouble today. It is these frontline workers, who are usually the least paid and least appreciated, who actually have the most influence day to day on your brand.

In my youth, I worked every front line job possible—from the gas station to restaurants, the movie theater to retail.[1] I understand the

---

[1] As Wayne said in *Wayne's World*, "I have a large assortment of name tags and hairnets."

effect a motivated work force can have on a company, and in contrast an unmotivated one. And believe me, I was much more the latter.

My favorite of these jobs was at the Famous Players movie theater. Working there in my late teens, I made friends who are still my core group of friends today. However, Famous Players, just like most places that employ young workers had a problem—how would they get minimum wage earners to care about their jobs?

Awesome in business is more often than not, driven from the bottom up. Individuals bring their own personality and passion to their jobs and amazing things happen. When the awesome is embraced from the top down, the actions and attitudes of individuals become the culture of a company.

Sadly, my experience at Famous Players was definitely a "what not to do" lesson for me in business. When the movie *Maverick* (an awesome poker, old western style movie with Mel Gibson and Jody Foster) came out in 1994 my coworkers at the theater and I decided it would be fun to run our own promotion for it. We asked management for permission and got the go-ahead, which back then meant "as long as it costs no money and everyone does extra work on their own time, sure. Go ahead." We had a very charming and supportive management team, as you can see.[2]

We went ahead with our plan, excited and determined to turn our movie theater into a *Maverick* themed wonderland. We bartered with the local party rental place and got a Crown and Anchor game and traded movie passes to the local laser tag company in exchange for laser guns to run a "fastest draw in Oakville" competition. We even painted poker themed windows in front of the theater. We did all this outside of our regular work hours and on weekends, at no cost to the company, all on our own dime.

Opening night came and we were all decked out in our *Maverick* clothing, Western era dresses for the ladies and cowboy outfits for the guys. The event was a huge success. Customers and staff all loved it. We filmed the entire thing and submitted it with a report outlining everything we had done and all the amazing results to the theater head office. We had never been so proud of our jobs.

---

[2]I think they were hired on their ability to demotivate and their want for free popcorn and movie passes.

With the speed of the Pony Express with a broken leg, a reply came from the human resources department at the head office. They returned the video and the report, without comment, only with a check mark on the front page. That was it. Not even a freaking smiley face or a gold star.

We were crushed. All of that momentum and energy we'd found and shared had gone completely unappreciated. We had spent well over 100 hours and not even cost the theater one extra penny, created a successful event, and made them money. And they couldn't have cared less.

People are a funny species. We all think we're unique in what makes us successful in our industries, when in reality we all thrive off the same basic principles. We want to matter. We want to believe that we have a greater impact with the work that we do. And the minute we think that we don't, our carelessness comes to the surface. If your employees know they make a difference on a day-to-day basis, I can promise you that not only will they do their jobs better, but they will remain with your company longer. And awesome HR is the key to making all of that a reality.

When was the last time you praised your employees or coworkers or heard praise yourself? We need to do more than leave a check mark. . . .

Human Is Social

We need HR to be a catalyst for what employees can do better.

IN ORDER TO PROTECT our own backsides, we have a tendency to overpolicy things rather than creating helpful guidelines that could leverage our greatest asset: our employees. Problems occur when employees think that they are off the clock, or off the record. In reality, if you state who your employer is on Facebook, Twitter, or anywhere else online, then you represent that brand: 24/7, every day of the year.

Unfortunately, most of the time HR is involved on the negative side—with what employees are doing or can do wrong. Rather than focusing on the "what ifs" on the bad side, we need HR to be a catalyst for what employees can do better. This is especially true for social media and establishing guidelines to create opportunities for success, rather than trying to censor workers.

Employees have the ability to interact with customers daily, in person and virtually. So how do we, from an HR perspective, create opportunities for them to enhance our brand while still protecting

it as well? This is where social media guidelines, not a policy, come into play. Social media is relatively new and changing and growing so quickly. And because of that, employees need guidance, but not necessarily strict restrictions.

Social media should be a part of a set of general communication guidelines that help employees understand their valuable—in fact, critical—role within your company. A guideline should include a statement letting employees know that they are the brand. As my friend Amanda Hite[1] says, "If your employees are your strongest asset, why would we try to silence them?"

A common thread throughout all of the best social media guidelines I have read is that they set out to raise awareness among employees of just how influential their online communication could be, rather than trying to control what people say. Employees need to know that if they reveal their employer online, they will be influencing brand perception.

This does not give you, as an employer, permission to ask a potential employee for their Facebook, or other social media site log-in information, to find out what they're really like. That would just be creepy—unless, of course, you're ready and willing to give them your log-in information, in return.[2]

I find it ridiculous to see a Twitter bio that lists an employer and then states, "These opinions are my own." This does absolutely nothing to separate the things you write from who you represent. No matter what your bio says, if you tweet an offensive comment, there will be repercussions, both to you personally and to any company listed on your profile.

HR needs to be the catalyst for the three As of awesome, allowing our employees to be the best they can be in social media. The three As of business awesome are:

1. Authentic
2. Authority
3. Appropriate

---

[1] www.talentrevolution.net/.

[2] Yes, employers are actually starting to do this, and because there haven't been any cases yet to set precedent for laws against it, they are getting away with it.

What are you doing every day to help your employees show their authentic awesome online? How are you setting them up to be authorities/experts in their areas? And what are you doing to set guidelines to ensure their communications are in line with business and market values and appropriately matched? These are the questions you need to be asking yourself to ensure awesome HR.

When you consider guidelines for your business, or for yourself personally, I suggest applying the same guidelines to social media as you would to a networking event. When people know where you work, because you've disclosed it online, it's like walking around the event wearing a shirt with your company logo on it.

- Don't say anything you wouldn't want to see on a billboard with your logo and picture, with your boss, your client, and your mom driving by.
- Don't just talk about the company the entire time. Engage with people.
- Don't do it drunk. Seriously, that just never works out.

A great example of harnessing our frontline employee power using social media is the @TwelpForce account for Best Buy. With more than 50,000 tweets to their credit, you can see the power of harnessing an employee community to help customers in need.

The account, open for use by any of the company's employees, is a place where they can virtually assist customers in real time. Best Buy employees are encouraged to tweet from the account by signing up through the system using their employee IDs. They collectively use the account to answer questions, with each tweet signed individually at the end.

It's a really bold move to crowdsource your customers service, and it has won them numerous awards. With more than 3,000 employees accessing the account, HR ensures that each of them understands the company guidelines regarding social media. These guidelines prohibit sharing things like nonpublic financial data and customer personal information. The account has operated train wreck free over the years, showing on a grand scale that large brands and employees can find their happy place online—with great HR and guidelines to help everyone find their way.

Even with examples like this, many companies would rather their employees not use social media at all. Censorship cannot be the answer. Did you know that more than 50 percent of employers in the United Kingdom have banned Facebook in the workplace,[3] which I think puts them in line with North Korea when it comes to censorship. They claim the restriction is to prevent a distracted workforce and protect productivity, but that's not really the issue. Facebook didn't create distracted workers.[4]

A distracted workforce is an unmotivated workforce. If your employees are getting their jobs done, there is no harm in their communicating with others. Facebook is the new personal phone call at work, and the rules should be as such. They are not a problem unless they hurt productivity.

A further censorship issue happens when companies not only ban work use of social sites but also forbid employees to reveal their workplace on personal pages. I've never understood why any company would want to do this. Short of the secret arm of the secret service[5] refusing to allow employees to disclose where they work, this is just a ridiculous practice. If you are either ashamed of who works for you or scared of what they will say, you're doing business wrong. If you don't trust your employees you do not have a social media problem, you have a hiring problem.

One of the things I do advise companies to do when it comes to social media is to maintain ownership of the account. As we saw in the news recently, if the building of a Twitter account (or any platform online) becomes the endeavor of an individual employee, there can be an issue later in deciding who owns that following.

This issue was brought up in December 2011, when PhoneDog, a website about the mobile industry, sued former employee Noah Kravitz for $343,000 for continuing the use of a Twitter account the company claimed as its own. Kravitz was a product reviewer for PhoneDog for four years, and during that time, he created a Twitter account: @PhoneDog_Noah. Over time, he gained 17,000 followers with a variety of tweets, both professional and personal. When he

---

[3] http://tgr.ph/FacebookStat.
[4] Minesweeper did.
[5] Even this group uses Twitter, by the way: www.twitter.com/secretservice.

resigned in October 2010, he changed his Twitter account name to @NoahKravitz and continued to tweet with his followers. PhoneDog claimed that the account was created for the company, whereas Noah claimed it was just like creating a personal e-mail address. He said, "It's this melding of personal and professional which is why I have gained a modest following. Because it's not just the dry headline and link to something." Regardless of the outcome, this lawsuit raises the red flag. As companies we need to make sure that any accounts created on behalf of our companies are owned by our companies.

By their nature, online followings are often driven by individual personalities. You have to ensure that if the voice of your account leaves the company, you don't lose the brand's voice online. Clearly stating ownership from the beginning will prevent any issues when someone leaves.

For updates and more stories about HR UnAwesome, visit www.TheBookOfBusinessUnAwesome.com/HumanResources.

Lehigh Valley

As social media continues to grow and companies and institutions find their place within it, what is acceptable and not is always evolving.

I'VE ALWAYS said that brands with personality have a leg up in social media. However, we need to be careful about just how personal we can get.[1] Some of the most successful online brands got that way from showing a ton of personality. The key is matching the personality to the brand *and* the market. We need to take into consideration the values and touch points for our audience and be prepared to deal with any fallout if those lines or opinions are crossed.

When Vanessa Williams, social media specialist running the Lehigh Valley Economic Development Corporation tweeted the following, the public did not react kindly:

> We start summer hours today. That means most of the staff leave at noon, many to hit the links. Do you observe summer hours? What do you do?

---

[1] And I'm not just talking about people posting about their cleanse . . .

Letting their followers know the office would be cutting out a bit early on a Friday for some golf ended up being a poor choice for this employee. Since the group is partly funded by tax dollars, people felt leaving work, the work they were paying for, early to have some fun was unacceptable. She ended up being fired[2] because of the tweet, and the public was assured there were always enough staff members on hand for anything they might need done.

I personally find the reaction to be a bit heavy-handed. Go to any golf course on a Friday at 3 PM and you'll find lots of people who should be working. The lesson here is when your job is publicly funded, you need to be a bit more careful about what you say. In this situation, the personality was found to be out of line with the values of their customers. No one working late on a Friday likes to think his or her tax dollars are paying someone else to golf. As a "social media expert" you are going to be held to higher standards in the virtual world, and likely Williams should have thought twice about how the tweet might be received.

It is a pity, though, because I think she was trying to authentically engage their followers and start a lighthearted conversation. With politicians and entertainers regularly tweeting out much, much worse, the punishment seems to outweigh the crime. All Vanessa's firing does is make other public institutions shy about engaging online for fear of a backlash about every little comment. I would have suggested the office reply with an apology and explanation more inline with the severity of her mistweet. There were probably a whole lot of ways to handle the situation other than firing someone.

This is part of the challenge of incorporating social media guidelines into our companies, which we spoke about earlier. The rules are still being made. As social continues to grow and companies and institutions find their places within it, what is acceptable and not is always evolving. We need these guidelines in place before issues occur. Most of the time, online trip-ups are small, and sorting out how to manage them can be simple. Giving employees a list of topics that are off-limits for sharing and even a list of suggested questions they should ask themselves before clicking Update, Post, or Send are important steps that can prevent a lot of future messes.

---

[2]http://bit.ly/LehighFiring.

21

Outrage Is Contagious

*We've become a society of keyboard commandos, who by nature are
passive in person and aggressive online.*

OUTRAGE IS CONTAGIOUS. We catch it from one another, sometimes
for good and sometimes for bad. We all want to stand up for something.
The thing is, it's really difficult to stand up when you think you're all
alone. One of the benefits of the online world is that, through social
media, we can see other people getting involved and then join in the
cause. An issue you never knew existed, or didn't even care about
10 minutes ago, now shakes you to your core, all because the people
you know care about it. With them beside you, you share, retweet,
and spread information like a 1970s protestor marching toward the
Washington Monument.

Outrage can even force companies to change their policies for the
better. For example, in November 2011, Bank of America announced
that it decided not to add a $5 debit card fee after receiving a ton of

negative online feedback when they announced it was coming.[1] Social media not only levels the playing field by giving everyone a voice but can create a united voice—a loud one—that companies can't afford to ignore. As business owners, we need to be listening.

One of the things I love about social media is how people stand up for one another. The art of "having your back" has returned. The problem is, we tend to react before thinking, and that can turn standing up for someone into trouble—for ourselves, for our brands, and for everything in between. But we should never forget the fact that no person or business is perfect. We've become a society of keyboard commandos, who by nature are passive in person and aggressive online.

With companies, we would rather rant online than look for resolution from the business first. As business owners, I know we all make mistakes and we'd all appreciate the chance to right a wrong. If you've already read the Awesome side of the book, you will remember my Hilton story from the beginning. Think about that experience and how it would have gone differently if I hadn't complained to the waitress and just tweeted about my poor service. I could have simply tweeted that the food sucked and walked away, but the issue would not have been resolved and I wouldn't have learned that the chef cared about my experience.

I've seen people post on Facebook and Twitter about a terrible meal or bad service experience without ever having asked for it to be resolved, as though fear of the impending social media geek-tsunami would have Smurf unicorns running off into the night to fix it all. Let's give companies, and people, a chance first. The next time you're about to rage online, make sure you give the business a chance to make it right first. If the company fails to make it right, then on my command, unleash social media hell.

In the next few chapters we are going to look at outrage gone contagious, and gone very, very wrong in three different ways. First, we'll look at some folks who should have checked their facts better before speaking their minds and how, when they didn't, the world stood up together to protest (although on shaky ground). Then we'll look at some companies that should have known that outrage doesn't

---

[1] http://bit.ly/BankOfAmericaOutrage.

take the weekend off and how being absent from your wall or not monitoring online conversations about your brand can result in a small mistake becoming a full-on outrage geekalanche. And, finally, we'll look at the lost causes—companies that exemplify the fact that social media does not make a company good or bad by doing things online that no social media specialist can fix—and the outrage that followed.

Check Your Facts

What's the ROI of getting shot through the heart?

SOCIAL MEDIA IS AN AMPLIFIER. The little mix-ups and mistakes we all make in life are just part of being human, and usually we do them quietly. But when we fark up online, people are listening. Our mistakes can get a whole lot louder, which is why checking our facts before we share information online is really important. Before you fuss with your spelling and your grammar and before you click Update, Post, or Send, please make sure what you are sharing is valid. Or at the very least include in the comment that you aren't sure. So when you see on Twitter that Jon Bon Jovi is dead, maybe you will pause and think for a minute before you share.

In December 2011, news of Jon Bon Jovi's death spread online like a blaze of glory. The thing is, he wasn't dead. He was alive and well in New Jersey, as you can see in the awesome picture he posted of himself to quiet saddened fans (see Figure 22.1).

Figure 22.1   Jon Bon Jovi Alive and Well

Source: David Bergman/PSG. ©2011 David Bergman/DavidBergman.net. Used with permission.

The news had not started by accident, but by a disgruntled musician who decided to spread the little lie.[1] He was upset that Jon Bon Jovi has been focusing more on business than on music. He created a fake blog, which apparently was enough for people to believe the news was legit. Fans fell into mourning, believing that their favorite singer was not living on a prayer.[2] The man said openly later that he did not expect it to grow the way it did. And it never would have, if we all weren't so quick to pass the news along.

In the end, it all worked out for Bon Jovi. But think for a moment if you were part of his family or a friend and saw that news. What if the false information was about a fire at your kids' school or an accident on your wife's route home from work? The power of social media to spread news may be its greatest use for good, but it can also be a detriment. We need to think before we share.

This incident had some unexpected social media results, which are also really scary. The mistake made the name Bon Jovi trend on Twitter and brought him and his music back into the spotlight, potentially increasing album sales. I tweeted the picture shown in Figure 22.1, and it became one of my most popular tweets ever. I know in some boardroom right now, some guys are calculating the ROI of

---

[1] http://bit.ly/JonBon.
[2] Okay, I'll stop now. I'll go lay down on a bed of roses.

faking their deaths. What's the ROI of getting shot through the heart? We're all to blame. We give Twitter a bad name. Baaaad naaaame.

When we talk about best practices online, there are always the few who shout, "No rules!" But social media is a tool, and there are ways to use it that make it better and more effective, and checking our facts is at the top of the list.

When a rude customer decided to make a comment to his bartender about her weight, along with a zero tip, she decided to let her online world have a look and posted the receipt (see Figure 22.2) on her Facebook page.[3] She included his name, Andrew Meyer, as well.

At a certain point, the waitress, Victoria Liss, also posted a picture of the man she believed had left the "tip," except it was the wrong man. Then the cyber-witch hunt began, except everyone was looking for the wrong target.

Was the man right to leave a nasty comment to his waitress? Probably not. Was she right to post the receipt to Facebook? I don't see a problem with it. Was it okay to post a picture of someone without making sure it was of the right man? I'm thinking no.

It spread like wildfire. Most people at some point have worked in the food industry. I've done everything from serving the food, to cooking the food, to cleaning up after the food. Anyone who had ever had a rude customer had Victoria's back. Anyone who'd ever wanted to lose a few pounds rallied to her side. This man deserved to be virtually smacked for what he did. But we need to be careful when we

Figure 22.2   UnAwesome Receipt

---

[3] http://bit.ly/ReceiptUnAwesome.

are virtual vigilantes, because once we put something out there, we can't pull it back in.

One of the things that make the Internet so wonderful is how we can get empathy from other people, but we have to be careful about how far we go. With potential backlash, lawsuits, and consequences to our brand, instituting a one-hour wait before posting something is a smart move. It turns out a third guy named Andrew Meyer saw the story in the news and sent her a 100 percent tip because he didn't want his name being used in a bad way and thought she'd like that. I thought that was pretty awesome.

The need to check your facts is a responsibility that grows as your online influence increases. Although someone with a smaller following may be able to get away with a mistake or two, depending on who sees it, the more people you have watching what you say, the more risk you have of your mistake catching on. The ramifications of the mistake also get a whole lot worse depending on how sensitive the issue is. There's no better example of this—the culmination of platform size and issue sensitivity—than when Ashton Kutcher decided to tweet about the firing of football coach Joe Paterno.

After learning the news, he tweeted to his 8 million followers how upset he was that the Penn State coach had been fired. The thing is, he really should have checked the reasons behind the firing[4] before he clicked Update. In case you, like Ashton haven't heard, the coach was fired after it was discovered that he had been a part of covering up a decades-long history of child abuse at the school.

The online world was already outraged by the abuse scandal, and the tweet made it seem like Ashton was endorsing what had happened. The thing is, he wasn't. He was just behind in the news and thought the firing was because of something else. When he realized what had happened, he issued an apology and said he would stop tweeting until he figured out how to manage the results of his tweet.

He ultimately decided, and announced publicly, that he would be turning his account over to Katalyst, the PR company he helped found, to manage his tweets before they posted.

---

[4]http://onforb.es/PennStateMistweet.

Up until today, I have posted virtually every one of my tweets on my own, but clearly the platform has become too big to be managed by a single individual. When I started using twitter, it was a communication platform that people could say what they were thinking in real time and if their facts were wrong the community would quickly and helpfully reframe an opinion. It was a conversation, a community driven education tool, and opinion center that encouraged healthy debate. It seems that today twitter has grown into a mass publishing platform, where ones tweets quickly become news that is broadcast around the world and misinformation becomes volatile fodder for critics. . . . A collection of over 8 million followers is not to be taken for granted. I feel responsible to deliver informed opinions and not spread gossip or rumors through my twitter feed. While I feel that running this feed myself gives me a closer relationship to my friends and fans I've come to realize that it has grown into more than a fun tool to communicate with people.

I don't actually agree with his decision here or with his statement fully. This has nothing to do with what Twitter has become and more about the subject he was addressing. Community is not about unconditional support, especially when the community has no barrier to entry. Your followers are not necessarily your friends, and it's not like a group e-mail that goes out to only your contacts. Twitter has always been, and always will be one thing, a conversation platform. But we don't get to choose what conversation people want to have with us.

To wrap it up, online public proclamations without confirmation of facts are not like messing up a song lyric while singing in your car. It can hurt your brand, and potentially even lead to a lawsuit. Nobody is perfect, but instead of trying to be first to spread something around, try to be the first to confirm it. Otherwise, you could go down in a blaze of glory.[5]

---

[5] I'm so sorry. . . .

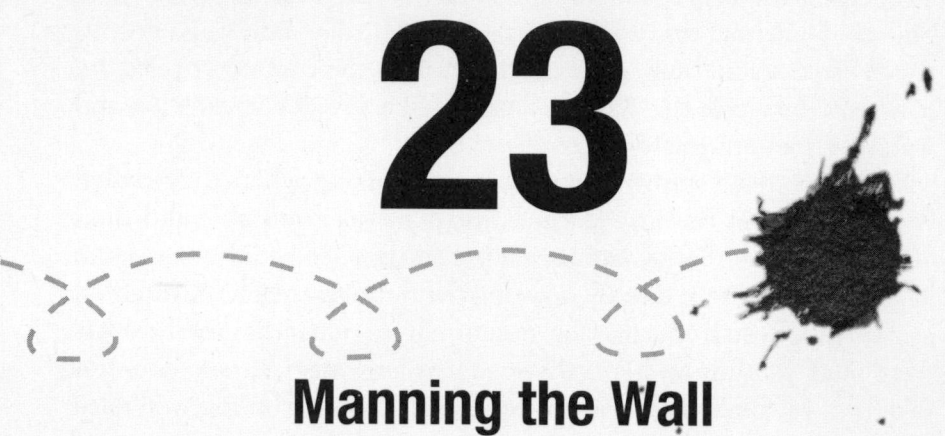

23

Manning the Wall

Outrage does not take the weekend off.

YOU KNOW WHAT PHOTOGRAPHERS don't like? When you say they are only as good as their cameras. You would think that a camera company would know that—or at the very least consider the ramifications of posting it on their Facebook page (see Figure 23.1).

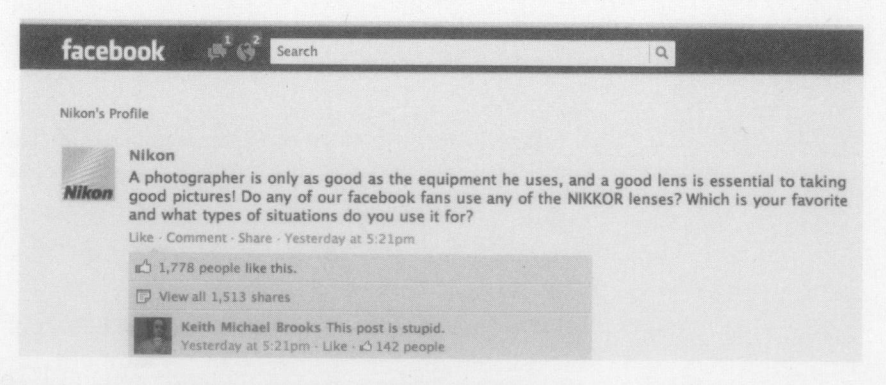

Figure 23.1   Nikon Facebook Status Update

I think the first comment should have been a bit of a red flag for Nikon about how this was going to go. And they didn't just post it; they posted it and then left it to sit there. As the comments piled on, it was shared across the Web, and people like me took screenshots and watched the outrage grow.

I'm not really sure what they were thinking when they posted the comment in the first place. Clearly, it was a mistake, and their audience did not appreciate it at all. The thing is, it did not have to become as crazy as it did. By ignoring the outrage, they let it catch on and spread. Even in the first few minutes, it was clear that their readers were mad. Within an hour, the rage was growing. Outrage does not take the weekend off. If you are going to be present online, you need someone manning your wall.

I know what you're thinking. "Scott, I can't possibly be online 24/7 watching the Internet for rage." Of course not. I understand that we all need to sleep and that businesses have hours of operation. But then please, *please* don't post something just as you're running out the door! Why ask a question, like Nikon did, and then not be there to listen to the answer? All it shows is that you don't care—about the answer or the people commenting. This is one of the biggest problems with a business Facebook page. People have been taught correctly that Facebook uses an algorithm called EdgeRank to prioritize updates in order of engagement levels, so the more likes and comments on a status update that a brand has, the more it gets shared in the News Feed. Brands see this, and they smartly ask an open-ended question; I do it all the time. But to ask a question like this and then not be around for the answers is a recipe for disaster. Leaving your computer for a few hours online is like leaving the real world for two weeks.

And your absence means that if things go bad, they could go Nikon bad.

Manning your wall means making sure you are watching the conversation and being part of it. It means protecting your brand page from spam and hate. This does not mean to delete negative feedback or comments. Those need to be managed and replied to. If you take the conversation off public space, you need to be sure to close the conversation publicly so that other readers can see you aren't ignoring comments. A simple reply asking someone to DM, send you an e-mail,

or call in will show that you are actively listening and working on whatever the issue may be.

When ChapStick launched a new campaign, featuring the image of a woman from behind looking for her missing ChapStick in the sofa, they could never have expected the rage that was coming.[1] A blogger saw the ad, found it offensive, and decided to share her feelings on the brand's Facebook page. Rather than replying or dealing with the negativity, ChapStick deleted the comments. More and more people went to Facebook and posted negative comments. ChapStick deleted those, too. This kept going until there were so many comments, going up so quickly, that ChapStick couldn't keep up and the comments started showing up on their wall.

The campaign was called, "Where do lost ChapSticks go? Be heard at facebook.com/chapstick." *Be heard.* How amazing is that? The funny thing about asking your audience a question, especially for feedback, is that sometimes they answer. And you need to be prepared to hear them. The ad isn't really offensive. What would have happened here, if left up, is that a few uptight people would get their ChapSticks in a knot and then the company's brand defenders would jump in to defend ChapStick and say the things they can't say as a brand, like "Relax" or "You need to get out more." Instead they poked the virtual bear by deleting comments, trying to silence the voices. The outrage grew because ChapStick refused to listen to anyone. And it grew louder and louder until it could no longer be ignored.

As a brand, if you're going to ask for conversation, you need to allow it instead of burying your head in the sand . . . or in this case, the sofa.

---

[1] http://bit.ly/ChapstickUnAwesome.

24

Franklin Goose

The only thing worse than a geek-tsunami is a momalanche.

WHEN A COMPANY CALLED FRANKLIN GOOSE decided to encourage bloggers to review products for their site by rewarding them with online credits, they probably thought it was a brilliant idea. For each review, they agreed to pay $5, which could be used on their site for purchases (see Figure 24.1).

FranklinGoose
We were not so clear in our last post! We are letting you have all the baby products you want for free. The trick is that every time you write a review we will give you $5 in store credit. The more reviews you write, the more credit you build. You see? You can use your credit to buy any product you want on our site: car seats, mattresses, diapers, shampoos, furniture, etc. This offer is valid until March 31st.

March 20, 2010 at 7:22am

👍 48 people like this.

Figure 24.1   Franklin Goose Facebook Status Update

They clearly replied to questions and clarified that there was no maximum number of reviews someone could submit and that they would be paid for each one. The credits might take a bit of time to show up on their accounts, but only because they wanted to make sure no one was sending in duplicates or trying to trick the system in any way.

So, what happens when you offer to pay, without a maximum? People send in reviews! It worked, right? Problem is, it worked so well that the company couldn't keep up. By March 26, just six days after the post shown in Figure 24.1, they were asking reviewers to "bank" their credits, offering "20% if you postpone and bank your store credit between 6 months and 1 year."

Being bombarded by angry reviewers, they eventually sent out an e-mail, letting everyone know that they would not be able to make good on the promotion. The reviewers were furious.[1] They believed that the company clearly saw the offer was spinning out of control and should have stopped it right away. Bloggers dug into the company's information and found out that even though they presented themselves as a small company, they were actually much larger. Before the promotion, they had actively and publicly offered to pay someone for a marketing idea that would "go viral," showing that they had an understanding of the nature of what was happening with their promotion.

The response from some people was, "What's the big deal?" They were virtual credits; the company removed the reviews. That's not the point. Outside of the basic principle of not standing behind an offer, the website gained better search engine rankings, exposure to each reviewer's social circle, and back links from their blogs. The business moral of the story applies across any crowdsourced contest or project: you need to cap the number of entries/submissions/prizes to an amount you can manage. This means you won't have to back out of the offer, thereby outraging your audience. Plus it actually helps with creating scarcity. If you do screw up and you see the wave about to crash, start fixing the problem within hours, not days or weeks. The only thing worse than a geek-tsunami, is a momalanche. They will bury you.

---

[1] http://thesavedquarter.com/2011/03/franklin-goose-you-suck/.

25

Boners BBQ

Social media doesn't make a business bad or good; it amplifies what they already are.

Just 10 days into 2012 already an epic story of outrage had caught my eye. UnAwesome reader, sometimes outrage online is just so easy and justified, it's impossible to stop. When businesses make mistakes and the outrage begins, sometimes we can feel badly for them. We all make mistakes, right? Other times, as was the case with Boners BBQ in Atlanta, the online interaction is just so rude and out of line, all we can do is get angry along with the crowd.

Let's say you own a BBQ joint and a customer comes in, one of the only ones you have that day, and orders a meal. You can tell she's not happy, and it ends up being verified by a well-written and factual review on Yelp.

You see the review and have a few choices in front of you of how you can react. So what do you do to make it right?

a. Get in touch with her and offer a meal for free to make it up.
b. Respond to the Yelp review by apologizing and explaining the issues.
c. Call her a bitch and post her pic on Facebook.

If you picked c, then you may have a new fave BBQ joint to hang out at!

Here we go, ready? Buckle up your brisket:[1]

- Stephanie and her husband go to Boners BBQ in Atlanta for a meal after grabbing a $10 off coupon from Scoutmob.
- They leave, and she posts her review on Yelp—one of the better-written reviews on the site to be honest. She lists the things she liked and didn't like, with reasons why. Not an all-caps "ZOMG!! THIS PLACE IS HORRIBLE!"
- After seeing the Yelp review and being told she didn't tip the server, the person who runs the Boners BBQ Facebook page decides to put her in her place by posting her picture (see Figure 25.1). (The censoring was done by me; they posted the unedited photo.)

Figure 25.1   Photo Posted on Facebook

And they added both the description and follow-up comment shown in Figure 25.2.

---

[1]Special thanks to Johanna Harrison and Michael McCready for the screenshots and heads up.

Boners BBQ
NOT WANTED! (Stephanie S.) left waitress 0.00 tip on a $40 tab after she received a Scoutmob discount. If you see this women in your restaurant tell her to go outside and play hide and go fuck yourself! Yelp that bitch.

Like · Comment · Share · 17 hours ago

👍 33 people like this.

🔁 28 shares

 Andrew Capron forgot to mention bitch cleaned her plate...every last drop!
17 hours ago · Like · 👍 1

Figure 25.2   Boner's Facebook comment #1

Source: Captured by Johanna Harrison. Used with permission.

- So, like most places on the Internet, the morons were there first saying things like "F&$K YA!" and other eloquent expressions, clicking "Like" to share it with their other Grade 10 classmates. Then people started commenting on how it's wrong to post her picture and call her names, and they replied with remorse and maturity . . . just kidding, they told those people to "F&$# Off", too (see Figure 25.3)!

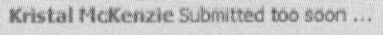 **Kristal McKenzie** I'm so glad you posted this! Now I (as a person who DOES tip well) know what restaurant to never, ever visit.

How do we know she even GOT good service? Based on the word of your "lovely" staff, I suppose? Maybe one of your staff made a horribly rude comment like some of the ones above while she was there. Or maybe she got wonderful service and left a cash tip - I often do this myself to help the servers get the full value - only for someone else to steal it off of the table.
9 hours ago · Like · 👍 49

 Kristal McKenzie Submitted too soon ...

Or maybe she genuinely did not leave a tip after getting wonderful service; which I agree is unfortunate. But definitely not worth the disgusting display you have sanctioned here.
9 hours ago · Like · 👍 30

 Kristal McKenzie OH! Now I get it -- she left you guys a negative review on Yelp. HAHA.
9 hours ago · Like · 👍 19

 Boners BBQ Hey Kristal McKenzie, go outside and go play fuck yourself
9 hours ago · Like · 👍 2

Figure 25.3   Boner's Facebook comment #2

Source: Captured by Johanna Harrison. Used with permission.

- Now the owner jumps in, to bring some logic and sanity to it (see Figure 25.4).

> **Andrew Capron** first of all, I (owner) was there, the restaurant had one table, the server (9 yrs exp,) had given the table her undivided attention. Ms. S. proceeded to tell the server how she could make every item she ordered better herself. Thirdly she cleaned her plates as if it was her last supper and then walked out leaving no tip. If anyone can justify that kind of behavior please do not come to Boners BBQ. As far as the Yelp review it's a forum for people to leave their comments justified or not...well this is our forum!
>
> 8 hours ago · Like · 👍 4

Figure 25.4   Owner's Comment

Source: Captured by Johanna Harrison. Used with permission.

- The logic of "She left us a bad review on Yelp, so we can say what we want on our wall!" really pushes the public's buttons, and a mass of comments hit their wall in response. Your wall or not, nothing can stop the geekalanche once it starts.
- They pull the entire status and comments and also delete any other posts that come in about it, which just makes people angrier. They eventually post an "apology," which is what I'd advise a client to do, just not one so . . . well . . . insincere (see Figure 25.5).

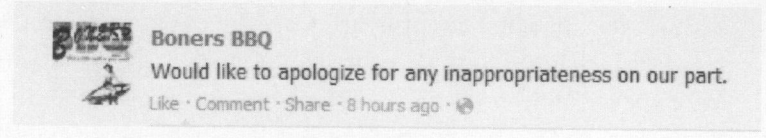

> **Boners BBQ**
> Would like to apologize for any inappropriateness on our part.
> Like · Comment · Share · 8 hours ago ·

Figure 25.5   Boner's First Apology

Source: Captured by Johanna Harrison. Used with permission.

- You just get this feeling that they're not apologizing for what they did but that they wanted to stop the mass amount of anger.
- It becomes pretty clear the apology was insincere when they commented on their original apology post later (see Figure 25.6).
- Yeouch. He had it perfect, explained what they've been doing, got frustrated, and had a bad "moment." Annnnd then reminded everyone there is no excuse for not tipping. What he doesn't understand is it's not about tipping or not (although if a tip is

Boners BBQ There was not a tip left, the fact of the matter is that my entire crew has been working practically free for 8 mos because we know we have something special. After not leaving a tip and the review I lost my lid and made a bad judgment in anger. There is no excuse for my behavior and there is no excuse for not tipping- Sincerely Andrew Capron

7 hours ago · Like · 👍 4

Figure 25.6 Apology Amendment

Source: Captured by Johanna Harrison. Used with permission.

mandatory, then it's a fee and should be stated as such); it's about how you deal with people. We are a forgiving society if you just own up. FedEx is a great example of that.

- As it turns out, she said she *did* tip. She posted on Reddit about the experience:

> That Facebook post was about me. That picture is me. I can give some background on this if anyone wants to know. The basics are that my husband and I went to Boner's BBQ for his birthday dinner. We were enticed there with a Scoutmob coupon (for $10 off) and we were the only ones in the place for our meal except for a brief period where a couple came in to get a pickup order. We paid in cash and yes, we left a tip. The ticket was $40 even minus $10 for the coupon + tax= $32.80 We dropped two twenties on the table and left. And yes, I did, politely, let the waitress know that the food wasn't as I expected and no, I didn't lick the plates or even eat all the food, that was my husband. He is far less picky about his BBQ than I am.

So what can we take from this? This isn't a "social media" problem. You don't train people not to call customers a "bitch" on Facebook and post their picture.[2] Social media doesn't make a business bad or good; it amplifies what they already are.

So realizing the error of their ways, or maybe it was the fact that news cameras showed up at their place and that *Huffington Post* blogged

---

[2] I'm picturing George Costanza saying, "Was that wrong?"

about it, they decided to give a little more sincere apology...but not really (see Figure 25.7).

Boners BBQ

Dear, Stephanie S. - We are truly sorry, it was a bonehead move on our part. But more importantly - it was rude to you and an inappropriate use of social media, which has been a driving force for our business because we can't afford traditional advertising. We rely on word-of-mouth. Your experience was yours to share and not mine to abuse. Boners BBQ is my passion and my life. Please give me the opportunity to serve you again at our expense- if not please allow me to fully refund your money on me, Sincerely, Andrew Capron."

Like · Comment · Share · 6 hours ago · 🌐

Figure 25.7   Apology after the Geekalanche

Source: Captured by Johanna Harrison. Used with permission.

Looks pretty good, right? And that's that! Problem solved...Or not.

Next someone adds this comment (Figure 25.8).

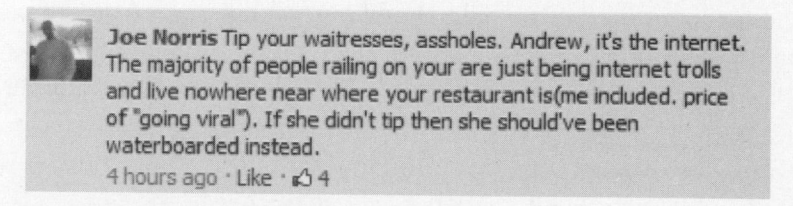

Joe Norris Tip your waitresses, assholes. Andrew, it's the internet. The majority of people railing on your are just being internet trolls and live nowhere near where your restaurant is(me included. price of "going viral"). If she didn't tip then she should've been waterboarded instead.

4 hours ago · Like · 👍 4

Figure 25.8   Facebook Comment

Source: Captured by Johanna Harrison. Used with permission.

Not sure what's the worst part here: the fact that he calls people "assholes," the fact that the woman actually *did* leave a tip (20 percent, at that), or the waterboarding. Yeah, you're right...the waterboarding part. But this isn't Boners BBQ that wrote it; they can't control what some jackalope says on their wall, right? You see that little "thumbs up" sign with a "4" beside it? Let's see who the 4 people are who clicked "I AGREE! ME LIKE!" beside the asshole's waterboarding comment (Figure 25.9).

Would ya look at that....Doesn't make the apology seem so sincere now, does it?

Some people have asked what would I advise them to do if they were my client. The answer is that they never would be. No amount of

Figure 25.9   Would You Like Boner's BBQ?

Source: Captured by Johanna Harrison. Used with permission.

social media or marketing help would ever trump crappy product and a crappy attitude.

Customers should not be afraid to leave honest reviews for fear of being publicly humiliated.

And one of you has to explain to my family why I have nine screen shots on my desktop called "Boner." Thanks.

26

Cooks Source

Don't mess with geeks.

SOMETIMES ALL THE FANCY MARKETING and social media consultants in the world can't help a brand. Social media does not make a company good or bad; it just amplifies what they already are. Two things people online really hate are ignorance and entitlement, and you don't want to mess with geeks. Because once it starts, the geekalanche can't be stopped.

A perfect example of this comes from a publication called *Cooks Source*. It turns out that the woman running *Cooks Source* was taking recipes from all over the Internet and publishing them, minus the credit and any payment.[1] The whole thing started when one blogger, Monica Gaudio, found out that one of her articles had been copied,

---

[1]http://www.wired.com/threatlevel/2010/11/web-decries-infringement/.

without credit, by the magazine. She got in touch with the editor, Judith Griggs, and received the following, unawesome reply:

> But honestly Monica, the web is considered "public domain" and you should be happy we just didn't "lift" your whole article and put someone else's name on it! It happens a lot, clearly more than you are aware of, especially on college campuses, and the workplace. If you took offence and are unhappy, I am sorry, but you as a professional should know that the article we used written by you was in very bad need of editing, and is much better now than was originally. Now it will work well for your portfolio. For that reason, I have a bit of a difficult time with your requests for monetary gain, albeit for such a fine (and very wealthy!) institution. We put some time into rewrites, you should compensate me! I never charge young writers for advice or rewriting poorly written pieces, and have many who write for me . . . ALWAYS for free.

You know what writers don't like? When you steal their material, and then when caught, rather than apologizing and fixing the situation, you suggest that you're doing them a favor. Calling the Internet public domain, where anything can be taken by anybody, is false and insulting. And to top it off, telling the author how lucky she is that the magazine hadn't charged her for the editing done to the piece because it was so sloppy is evidence of some kind of nerve.

Well, the author shared this correspondence on her blog and asked the "public domain" of the Internet what they thought. The virtual tsunami that occurred was second to none. It wasn't just the fact that she was stealing content that got people so upset. It was her ridiculous response that sparked the fire. This got everybody in a tizzy—not just writers, but the general public. This escalated to the point that the magazine advertisers were contacted and asked to pull their support for a plagiarized magazine. *Cooks Source* was out of business two weeks later. Don't mess with geeks. We live in our mom's basement, and we have nothing else to do but stand up for one another.

27

Social Extortion

Publicity has always been valuable, but we all need to play by the same rules.

BLOGS, TWITTER, AND FACEBOOK have provided new platforms for voices all around the world to be heard. They've given people opportunities to become writers and/or reviewers about every topic known to humans. The perks that come with these can be anything from free swag at conferences to free products and trips. The problem is, when we, as bloggers and social media addicts, start having a sense of entitlement. I know I walk around saying, "Do you know who I think I am?" in my head all the time. But I never use that as leverage to get something for free. Don't get me wrong; I get free stuff all the time, but that's because they come to me.

This sense of entitlement has gotten so bad that I've heard of people threatening places that if they don't comp them rooms, meals, or swag at events, they will tweet, post, or give negative Yelp or Trip Advisor reviews. *These* are the people who need to be outed and have a

social media beat down. *They* are the ones who make the social media sphere bad for the rest of us.

As a business, if you think you are a victim of social extortion, what should you do? If you have a virtual paper trail, showing over e-mail that you've been threatened with bad reviews, hold on to it as proof. This way, if someone does go ahead and put up the negative review, you can contest it. Get in touch with the website hosting the comments, share the e-mail trail with them, and have it taken down. Sites want to maintain their integrity and take the value of their reviews seriously. It is as important to them, as it is to you, that the content on their site be valid and trustworthy.

If you do choose to comment back on a negative review, please take the high road and don't make it personal. This goes for any kind of review about a product, service, or company in general. I recently saw a bar owner on Yelp not only berate those making negative reviews but go on to publicly tweet to the commenters, challenging them to "say it to his face." I understand that building a business can make it feel very personal, but that is not an excuse to lose your cool online. Name-calling is always, always a bad idea. When we react personally, we come out looking badly every time.

I also don't recommend publicly shaming the blogger; all it does is make your brand look bad. But it's okay to stand up for yourself. This is also a good reason to have a virtual fan base; your fans will defend against these false accusations.

If you do want to leverage people's online influence, either work with an agency who uses its own analytics or use a tool such as Klout.com that will show truly just how influential someone is, not just how influential that person says he or she is. Just remember that all grading systems are subjective, and I really think the best equation is to work with influencers who are a natural fit for your brand and are fun and easy to work with.

If you find yourself getting hit up for free stuff, especially in a public forum where others are watching, request that the person follow the same procedure that any traditional media representative would. Send the person to a submission form on your website, where the individual can explain his or her credentials, what is being requested, and what his or her plans are if given a product for free. This will usually scare away 80 percent of freebie seekers, give you a database of people to

consider for the future giveaways, and close the conversation publicly, showing you're listening.

Publicity has always been valuable, but we all need to play by the same rules. Giving away free stuff to everybody who asks is a great way to lose your shirt.

For updates and more stories about public relations UnAwesome, visit www.TheBookOfBusinessUnAwesome.com/PublicRelations.

28

ConAgra

They wanted it to go viral, and oh boy, did it ever.

I'M SURE SOMEONE in marketing thought this was going to be an amazing idea: invite food and mom bloggers to an "exclusive and intimate" dinner in New York City and include a celebrity chef. Let them know they would be enjoying a delicious meal and encourage them to let their readers know just how excited they were about the upcoming event. "Allow" them to leverage their own readerships and share the upcoming experience with one of their readers as a guest. Bloggers love being able to give away prizes, right?

I bet they could taste the bonus that was coming their way.

The thing is, the bloggers were in for a surprise.[1] And they were not going to be happy about it. The dinner was a setup to launch two products: Three Meat and Four Cheese Lasagna and Razzleberry Pie, both made by Marie Callender's, a frozen line from ConAgra Foods.

---

[1] http://nyti.ms/ConagraUnAwesome

There were hidden cameras in the dining areas, ready to capture the bloggers' reactions—a plan put together by Ketchum, the public relations arm of the Omnicom Group.

When the bloggers realized what was going on, their reactions were less than positive. They were embarrassed for being tricked and for unknowingly bringing their readers along for the ride. They were furious. One blogger wrote that she "pointed out that the reason I ate organic, fresh and good food was because my calories are very precious to me, so I want to use them wisely . . . I'm NOT their target consumer and they were totally off by thinking I would buy or promote their highly processed frozen foods *after tricking me to taste it.*"

No one likes to be fooled.[2] These bloggers grew their online voices based on readers trusting their opinions. By encouraging them to share the story before knowing what was going on, they were forced to go public with being tricked or give a positive review to the dinner. Not a good corner to force a blogger into.

This is an example of reverse social extortion. The company has already benefited from the social momentum brought with this trip. They have given the bloggers no choice. They must either pretend they enjoyed it or admit they have been fooled, making them look stupid. I understand switching out one type of bottled water for another, or surprising people with something amazing, but something as sensitive as food quality to food and mom bloggers is not something to mess with. It just blows my mind.

They could have done the whole trip and told them ahead of time that it was for new lines of food and found writers who would have supported them. But instead they wanted it to go viral, and oh boy, did it ever.

[2]Reminds me of this Chris Farley clip: http://www.ebaumsworld.com/video/watch /1035969/.

800 Million Not Listening

Facebook is a place that is run by people who are there for themselves. It's a look at me platform.

ONE OF THE PROBLEMS WITH PUBLISHING a book is that we authors have to submit the content six to eight months before it's published. So me talking about the stats on Facebook right now in theory could make me look like a moron. So I'm just going to make some numbers up, and we'll call them estimates.

By the end of 2012 it is "estimated" that Facebook will have a billion users. I don't think I have to write a chapter that explains to you that Facebook is important. But what you do need to know is it's not as easy as you might think. Saying that Facebook is a good place for your market because of the numbers is like saying America is a good place to open a business because of its population. Yes, there are people there, but if you just open a store because there are people there you would be out of business very quickly.

Having a "presence" on Facebook is like having a website on the Internet. It's not being there that counts. It's what happens within the page. Different strategies are applicable depending on your business. If you are a well-known brand, one that is either mentioned a lot or has a large in-house customer list, you can simply promote the Facebook page on your existing platform and get 10,000 likes in a day. Then all you have to look at is a Facebook management program.

However, if you are an unknown brand, the billion people on Facebook may as well be one. That's what Facebook is: 1 billion people and nobody is listening. Facebook is a place that is run by people who are there for themselves. It's a look-at-me platform. This isn't a negative thing; it's a community of our friends and family. Opening your business page and having six likes on it a month later doesn't make you look very professional. That's why I never suggest that brands start out with a Facebook page.

Create momentum on a platform elsewhere and then expand onto Facebook once you have a following. To have a page just for the sake of having a page and not using it or monitoring it is worse than not having a page at all. The very numbers that we brag about in social media, of how big Facebook is, is one of its biggest deterrents. It's really hard to be heard in a crowded room.

If you are going to have your brand active on Facebook, you really need to understand EdgeRank, the algorithm that Facebook uses to populate people's pages.

Facebook defines EdgeRank as Affinity $\times$ Weight $\times$ Time Decay. Now, I know you were promised there would be no math in social media, but let's just look at this equation for a minute together and sort it out. It is a way of looking at the relationship between users and the pages they interact with. That can be with a like, share, view, post of a page to your wall, or even a comment. This is important for a business page, because it lets them see how fans are engaging with them. The most weight is put on not only how new the update is, but the engagement level (likes and comments). Your goal with your updates should be not only to be awesome but also to be the catalyst for conversation.

In a nutshell, Facebook rewards engagement. My man Jay Baer[1] calls it presumed relevancy, and it's the secret sauce of what goes into

[1] http://www.convinceandconvert.com/.

the News Feed. When any of us log into Facebook, our opening page is the main News Feed—usually a collection of shared cat videos, sappy pictures, and a hipster complaining about Facebook. The goal of the brand is to get its status update into this main feed. The best way to do that is to create engaging updates, ones that a number of people like, comment on, and share. So you posting an update about how much you want people to buy stuff from you won't get much traction. But asking an open-ended question or starting a discussion on something timely and topical will.

Now be careful, because just as we've learned data is dangerous and kids don't play on a crappy playground,[2] you will find research can be deceptive. No doubt you will find research from a social media scientist that claims that photos and videos get shared a lot more than text. But that's very misleading. *Awesome* photos get shared a lot. *Awesome* videos get shared a lot. And compelling updates get liked. It's not the *type* of update that you should focus on, but rather the content in it.

Like most things in business, being there is not the point. It's what we are doing that makes it work or not. Luckily, there are a few common things most brands are doing that have them falling flat on their Facebook pages. We're going to talk about these in the next three chapters.

---

[2]See Chapters 10 and 12, respectively.

30

5 Percent of Companies
Are Awesome

As a small company, one of the best things you can do is actively engage with commenters and fans to show you are listening while your larger competitors are not.

As I was doing my book research, one of the statistics I ran across, which both shocked me and yet didn't surprise me at all, was that 95 percent of consumer inquiries on brand Facebook pages aren't replied to in a timely fashion.[1] It's hard enough to get anyone to engage on your page in the first place, but if they do and you ignore them, one of two things will happen: (1) they just won't come back, or (2) they will come back with all-caps anger—neither of which do you want.

Social media needs to be treated like a customer service hotline, instead of like a letter that comes in the mail. A response time of 24 to

---

[1] http://bit.ly/FacebookReplies.

48 hours looks horrible in a public setting. It should actually be treated more urgently than a phone call, because other people are watching. When you ignore one comment, you are showing everyone who visits your page that you would ignore them as well. The perception is not only that you aren't listening but that you don't care about your customers in general. There is no "Currently our lines are busy; please hold" in social media. Even replying to a comment with, "We will look into this" or "We will e-mail you directly" shows publicly you are present and trying.

We don't bring our brands to the front of the crowd in Facebook by ignoring customers; it's that simple. You cannot look at fan numbers and make assumptions about who is seeing your posts. If all you do as a brand is use Facebook to push your sales and promotions, you will quickly get lost in the crowd. As a small company, one of the best things you can do is actively engage with commenters and fans to show you are listening while your larger competitors are not. If you are spending your time doing everything you can to increase fan numbers, while ignoring the ones holding up their hands with questions and feedback, you are making a huge, and very common, mistake.

31

Win a Chance to Ruin Your Brand

I would rather have 500 targeted new likes than 5,000 generic ones.

I UNDERSTAND WANTING to get more likes on your Facebook page, and having a contest to bring them in is a reasonable thought. Unfortunately, this is where the plan usually falls apart. Success isn't measured on Facebook simply by how many likes you have. Sure, it makes us feel all loved online and warm and fuzzy, but it doesn't really mean anything, especially if we got people to our page with an untargeted Facebook contest.

If you decide to give away something, such as an iPad, to a random person who likes your page, all you end up doing is getting a lot of "fans" who like free stuff but aren't targeted demographically or geographically. They aren't even there because of your company; they are there because of the prize. The likelihood of these likes becoming true fans, or even customers, is small.

Not to mention, most Facebook contests are against the terms of service within the site. You risk losing your Facebook page because

of it. Generally, contests need to be run through third-party apps, which unfortunately means anybody entering needs to allow those apps access to their profile, which is a great way to drastically lower your number of entries.

If you are a camera company, running a contest asking for photo submissions makes great sense. But if you are a bed and breakfast in Florida and end up with 10,000 entries from around the world, all because they want an iPad, what's the point? I would rather have 500 targeted new likes than 5,000 generic ones.

For a great example of Facebook contests gone wrong, I had to include this story from Ali Martell about her experience with Timothy's Coffee. You can check out more from Ali's blog here http://www.alimartell.com.

Oh, Timothy's Coffees of the World...

...I have a bone to pick with you.

As a frequent coffee drinker, pumpkin lover, and Keurig-owner, I was thrilled to see this seemingly too-good-to-be-true promotion.

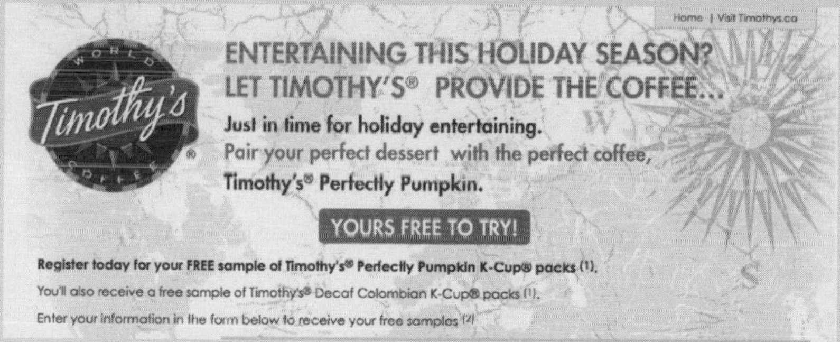

Figure 31.1

Free to try? Don't mind if I do.

All I have to do is GIVE YOU MY PERSONAL INFOR-MATION and you'll not only send me two boxes of Perfectly Pumpkin K-Cup packs, but you'll also throw in two boxes of Decaf Columbian K-cups.

Sure!

And then you sent me this:

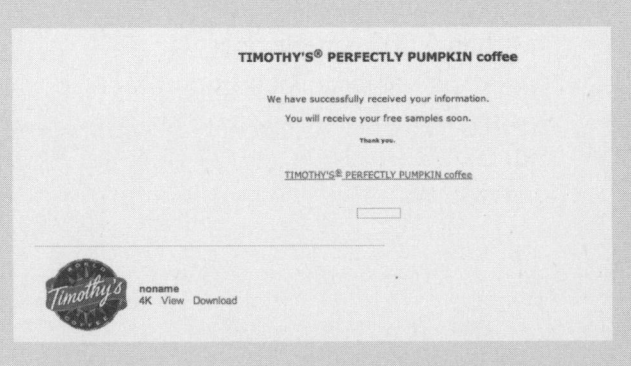

Figure 31.2

That right there?

That's called EMAIL CONFIRMATION that they have successfully retrieved my information and I would be receiving my samples shortly.

Only instead of receiving samples, I received this, in my inbox, just a few moments ago:

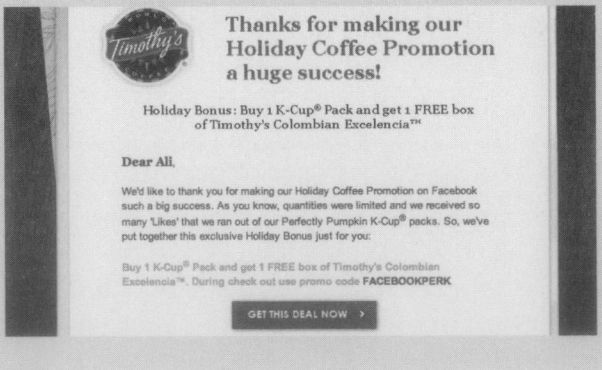

Figure 31.3

(continued)

(*continued*)

Let me get this straight, Timothy's.

You made me a promise that you couldn't keep.

So now, instead of holding up your end of the bargain, you would like to invite me to PAY FOR YOUR PRODUCT?

Interesting.

Very interesting.

And to top it all off, you currently have access to my email address AND my home shipping address, so that's awesome.

Well, I told your Facebook wall about how unimpressed I am.

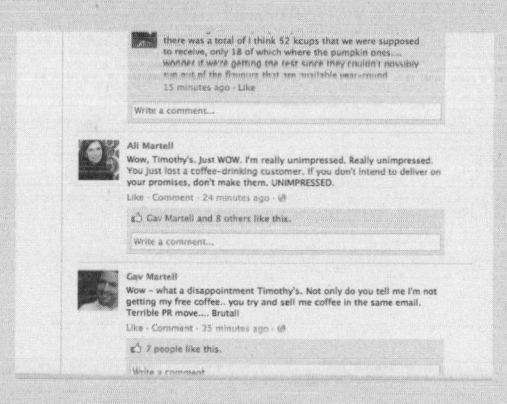

Figure 31.4

And judging by the way your Facebook wall is refreshing with new disgruntled customers . . .

. . . I'd imagine you are going to lose a LOT of customers today.

AND THEN, well, this is super fun little wrinkle. REMOVING all comments from your Facebook wall? Not cool, Timothy's. That simply makes you look worse. That lets me—and the hundreds of other disgruntled customers—know that you don't care about what we have to say. It seems there were at least ten different points in this process to swallow pride, grow a pair and make it right with customers. But you didn't. At all.

I hope it was worth it, Timothy's. I'm not *quite* sure this was the kind of publicity you were looking for.

And, just, you know, for the record. Since I'm sure there will be people screaming, "WOW! You are so selfish, Ali! Complaining about not getting your FREE stuff! How ungrateful can you get?!?!" please know that this has nothing to do with free stuff. That's not why I wrote the post. It's about a company behaving poorly. It's about a company lying to customers. It's about a company taking the personal information of many people. It's about a company not making good on promises. Timothy's—while I'm sure their intentions were very good and generous—should never have offered free product if they were not able to deliver. Timothy's—while I'm sure they planned to give out free product to everyone who got a confirmation email—needed to replace the product they couldn't deliver with something of equal value instead of a Buy One Get One coupon. End of story.

Source: Ali Martell, "Oh Timothy's Coffees of the World…" http://www .alimartell.com. Used with permission.

There are so many things wrong with the way Timothy's handled their contest. They asked for personal information and made a promise in return, which they then couldn't keep. And then, as with so many of our UnAwesome company stories, they failed to manage the outrage online and tried to delete and ignore it instead.

Like any interaction with our market, a Facebook contest is an opportunity to be awesome. The problem is, most of us are running them solely as a way to try to add as many likes as possible, with as little effort as possible. There are no shortcuts to building a following on Facebook, or any other platform.

How We're Killing Facebook

The most social, strongest community in the history of the world is filled with people who have become apathetic about events

THE BIGGEST THREAT TO FACEBOOK and its success isn't a change in format, structure, or infrastructure. It's user apathy—and more specifically when it comes to Facebook for business, event apathy.

Every single day I am invited to Facebook events that make me cringe. They may be 2,519 miles from where I live. They are for women. They are for Social Media for Beginners classes. It has gotten so bad that I don't even look at them anymore.

And I'm not alone in this. If you look at many of the pages for invites, you see numbers like these: 3 Yes, 19 Maybe, and 4,552 AWAITING REPLY!

Notice it doesn't show the number of people who said "No," which you should assume is about 400, since they most likely used a script to auto-invite 5,000 "friends" to the event.

Do the math.

It's not even the 400+ people you've pissed off with your untargeted invite to get three yes responses which you've actually achieved the impossible with: you've made direct mail and cold calling success ratios look good. It's the 4,552 who never even saw the invite that scares the bejeesus out of me.

This isn't a freak occurrence. Most people I've talked to have gotten so overwhelmed with Facebook invites to events like these that they've either stopped noticing invites or turned off notifications altogether (like I have). And that's horrible.

I threw a party at BlogWorld last year: open bar, 100+ of my fave people, fancy pants, velvet rope. Forty-five people on the invite list never even replied and didn't know about the event because they stopped checking them long ago. They missed an event that was targeted (only people I knew/thought were going to Blog-World were invited), and most would have come had they seen the invite.

And we have done this. The most social, strongest community in the history of the world is filled with people who have become apathetic about events. This has to stop.

Many people have said to me, "It's no big deal; just reply with no, and be done!" To that, I say, "NO." The onus to stop Facebook event spam should not be on the receiver. The logic is the same that e-mail spammers use (if you don't want it; just delete).

We need to stop:

- Inviting people to a local event if they aren't local.
- Creating events that aren't actually events but a way to e-mail mass numbers of people at once, regardless of reply.
- Constantly e-mailing people who haven't replied yet with information about your event as they have confirmed they are coming.
- Publicly inviting people to a private topic event (weight loss, confidence, being single). I've been invited to 15 different weight loss events in the past three months. What are you trying to say?

As we wrap up the Facebook section, I want you to be thinking about Facebook as something that can be a brilliant tool for your business—if you first understand why it is so popular in the first place. Facebook is a community; it's kind of like our life online. Here, we

have our friends and family all sharing stuff with one another, whether it be a post, picture, event, or product that we like.

As a brand on Facebook, you are trying to get into a circle of people, who for the most part don't really want you there. So you need to be very careful to ensure that people are spreading the word to one another about you, rather than you shouting it at them. That is the key to true Facebook success as a business: making the product and content so great that people want to share it themselves. The goal is not seeing how loud you can shout or how many likes you can get by giving away prizes.

The individual goes to Facebook for family and friends, not for sales pitches, and when they do decide to engage with companies, they are being ignored. All of this has created an abundance of apathy on the site; the numbers make it look like we shouldn't even try to be there.

The thing is, all this apathy means there is a whole lot of opportunity out there for you to be amazing. When everyone else is sucking at Facebook, that's your window to be awesome.

33

Hall of Shame

An apology or a firing, the best social media expert in the world, cannot undo this kind of malfeasance.

LIKE ANY HALL OF FAME, the Hall of Shame has certain criteria you need to meet if you want to be immortalized. To get your company's plaque, etched in infamy, you usually need to possess one, if not more, of the following criteria:

- **Ignorance:** The definition of *ignorance* is "lack of knowledge, education or awareness." And when it comes to most brands' awareness of the power of today's customers, ignorance is done to perfection. Back in the old days, which some businesses would call the glory days, a customer who had a problem with you may have told five people. Now this one complaint can reach 5 million, without exaggeration.

  Companies that keep behaving with such a flippant attitude toward customer service are a train wreck waiting to happen. They

need to be taking each and every customer experience seriously, as if it can potentially reach their entire current and potential market. Because it can.

- **Offensiveness:** Everybody is capable of offending somebody. But it takes an "extra special" somebody to be Hall of Shame offensive. I'm talking about being Third Circle Offensive, where what you have said or done, online or offline, is so bad that people not even remotely involved with the incident are shocked. They take their shock and share it with others.

  This type of offensiveness becomes more than about what one person said and becomes the representation of the brand itself. No apology or firing, or even the best social media expert in the world, can undo this kind of malfeasance.

- **Unaccountability:** I truly believe that we are a forgiving society. We give second chances, and we want to forgive—but only if the people/brand own up to their mistakes. Scapegoating, deflecting, or delaying remorse is a great way to turn the public against you. When you take a mistake and try to turn it into your next 30 percent off promotion, you're doing business wrong.

Take all of these, sprinkle in a little bit of horrible timing and me taking screen shots, and you may find yourself in the Hall of Shame. Many brands tried to reach the Hall since my first book came out, but it takes more than just a general distain for their own customers to be at the pinnacle of crapiness. Ladies and gentlemen, I present to you the inductees to the Business Hall of Shame.

Please hold your boos until the end.

For updates and more stories from the Business Hall of Shame, visit www.TheBookOfBusinessUnAwesome.com/HallOfShame.

34

Kenneth Cole

Sensitive times are not appropriate for humor or promotions.

ONE OF THE MOST AMAZING THINGS about social media, and Twitter especially, is how it's used during world events to share news in real time. When the news is bad, people rally together, supporting one another and getting the word out. We no longer have to wait for news to hit traditional channels; people are sharing their experiences now.

A brand misusing social media tools is one thing that really gets my goat.[1] Our first nominee for the Hall of Shame is Kenneth Cole,[2] not just the brand Kenneth Cole, actually Mr. Cole himself. This example also serves as a reason behind the hesitation of most PR people to allow the heads of companies to communicate directly with the public.

Mr. Cole may have thought it was humorous, timely, or just a great opportunity to promote their spring collection when he decided

---

[1] I don't even know what that saying means, but let's go with it.
[2] http://bit.ly/KennethColeUnAwesome.

Figure 34.1   Kenneth Cole Tweet

to hijack a trending topic of #Cairo. The hashtag was created around
a world event: protests and riots in Egypt. Now, hijacking trending
topics on Twitter is nothing new. But it's mostly done by spammers,
who put a popular search term in a tweet to get you to click. But this
is rarely done by recognized brands, let alone on a sensitive topic like
a riot. Which is what happened (see Figure 34.1).

As you can guess, an apology followed, the PR machine took over,
and life went on. There is a time and place for jokes. But there are
some topics that you need to leave alone—unless, of course, you want
a backlash like the one Kenneth Cole experienced.

Sensitive times are not appropriate for humor or promotions. It's
just in bad taste, and you will always come out looking insensitive.

Kenneth Cole is certainly not alone in committing this social
media crime. Another similar example of this was when the Italian
cruise ship *Costa Concordia*, carrying more than 4,200 passengers, ran
aground on January 13, 2012. The news hit Twitter fast. In light of
the seriousness of the event, you would assume the company was busy.
This should be the time when they are doing whatever possible to
make sure people on the ship and their families are taken care of as
well as possible. The thing is, on top of refunds, the company offered
a little bit more: a discount on future bookings for anyone affected.
Come on now.

The restaurant chain KFC got in a ton of trouble for posting this
insensitive status update on their Facebook page after an earthquake
struck Indonesia:

"Let's hurry home and follow the earthquake news. And don't
forget to order your favorite KFC menu."

The update was taken down and apologies were made by the company,

Microsoft made a similar misstep when they included a pitch for their new search engine in tweets about raising money to help people affected by the earthquake in Japan.

I can't stress enough how inappropriate a time it is to do this. Now is not the time to think about your sales numbers for next quarter. Now is not the time to think about recovering your brand image or what's next for your business. When you are in the middle of a crisis, you need to focus all your time and energy on the seriousness of the event and be respectful of everyone involved.

35

Newt Gingrich

You can't fake the true value that comes from an organically built, engaged following.

WHEN THE NEWS BROKE that Newt Gingrich allegedly bought the majority of his massive following on Twitter,[1] I was overjoyed and angry at the same time. Overjoyed, because I figured, "Ha! That's how he got more followers than me!" And angry, because it was just another example of people doing anything they can to get the perception of popularity online.

There are few things out there, few e-mails or scams, that cross my radar and get me angrier than ones that promise "followers fast!" The idea of tricking the system to make it look as though you have a platform goes against the very reasons to build one in the first place.

The situation made me even angrier because I think having politicians on Twitter and engaging online is such a great thing. I love

---

[1]http://gawker.com/5826645/.

how social media levels the playing field and gives everyone a voice. I hate that he was using inflated numbers to seem more engaged than his competitors. It's really top-level skeezy in my opinion. Which is why we find him here in the Hall of Shame.

So I was ranting to myself about the whole situation when I read the following post from my friend Jay Baer at www.convinceandconvert.com, and it made me look at this issue differently. I really couldn't say it any better than he did, so I wanted to include his words below.

5 Reasons Social Media Measurement Is Making You Lie to Yourself

With over 1.3 million followers, it would seem that this presidential hopeful has really won people over. Well, that would be the case, as @newtgingrich has more followers than any other GOP candidate. But word spread that Gingrich's team may have paid for fake followers, with the majority of his flock being inactive or dummy accounts created by follow agencies. Not the best press for someone running as a genuine candidate.

Social media measurement causes unsavory (and ineffective) marketing behavior because unlike the rest of our marketing key performance indicators, social media metrics are out there for anyone to see.

Was it a surprise last week when Presidential wannabe Newt Gingrich was (allegedly) busted for having 1.3 million followers on Twitter, most of which were bots and fake accounts? Not really. It may have raised an eyebrow that someone applying for the most important job in the world would (allegedly) stoop to fakery to boost follower counts. But despite some initial reluctance, politics has embraced the social media Egosystem as much or more than any other industry.

Being a former political consultant myself, this kerfuffle got me pondering about social media measurement and the bigger lessons of key performance indicators. I see five.

(continued)

(*continued*)

1. Visibility of Social Media Metrics Drives Behavior

How much do you think we'd be talking about twitter followers or Facebook likes if how many you have wasn't attached to your public profile like a goiter?

If on every website you visited you saw a number in the corner that showed how many email newsletter subscribers they had, we'd be putting a lot more emphasis into our email programs. **We care about twitter followers and Facebook likes disproportionately not because of the power of the medium, but because we keep score in public.**

There was a time when there was a lot of news coverage of comparative website "hits" but largely that kind of "story" went away with the fortunate exit of hit counters pinned to the footer of your site. Everyone knows that data from Nielsen, Compete, Quantcast, Alexa and their ilk is only semi-accurate unless the site chooses to report actual numbers, so we've mostly accepted the fact that website traffic is a dull topic not worth our curiosity or bile.

2. Our Belief That Bigger Is Better Makes It So

Every legitimate social media consultant in America will tell you that it's **not about how many twitter followers or Facebook likes you have, it's what you do with them**.

In terms of driving measurable behavior, conversions, revenue, loyalty and advocacy, etc. they are of course correct. Number of twitter followers doesn't mean a thing, right? Wrong.

The reality is that social media measurement is a very public dick measuring competition, and we buy it hook, line, and sinker. Why would Newt not only (allegedly) pay to build a following that dwarfs the other candidates, but then have the audacity/stupidity to brag about the advantage?

Because it matters in the court of public perception. Twitter is used monthly by just 8% of Americans 12 or older, according to Tom Webster and Edison Research, yet the penetration rate amongst "thought leaders" "celebs" and "media" is damn near

100%, and that drives its role as an arbiter of popularity and fame.

We may not like it. We may not even choose to admit it. **But it's disingenuous to suggest that the number of twitter followers has no impact on how you or your organization are viewed by the vox populi.** It's not a key performance indicator, it's a key popularity indicator.

3. You're Not Much Better Than Newt Yourself

Yes our fascination with the public nature of social media measurement causes some issues. But the bigger problem is that the whole system is a house of cards.

Guess what? **While most of your Twitter followers are probably real people they probably don't see your tweets, much less respond to them.** It's stunning how many marketers—even in major companies and agencies—don't understand (or choose to ignore) the massive difference between twitter followers and actual twitter reach.

If you have 10,000 followers, do 10,000 people see your tweet? Absolutely not. Many of those people do not use Twitter any longer (abandonment rates have been reported to be as high as 50%), may not be logging on to Twitter today, may not be logging on at a time where your tweet shows up in their timeline, or may use Twitter as a "social telephone" paying attention primarily to @replies.

The reality is that we do not know how many impressions each Tweet generates. We can determine engagement rate via clicks and retweets (I use Convince & Convert sponsor Argyle Social for social communication because of their incredible metrics). But, we cannot determine impressions, because Twitter will not show them to us. Hmmm, I wonder why?

Think about it from an email perspective. Twitter followers is the number of subscribers you have. Twitter reach (impressions) is your open rate, and that's not available.

(*continued*)

(*continued*)

A bunch of Newt's followers are (allegedly) robots. But the **net effect of a robot and an actual person that didn't see your tweets is exactly the same.**

4. Facebook Likes Is Just as Bogus

To their credit, Facebook at least shows us actual impressions in their Insights social media measurement console.

But the reality is that in our zeal to accumulate as many "likes" as possible for our fan page (largely comprised of people that already like us, so we're putting forth extreme effort to preach to the converted), we mostly **neglect to notice that a very small percentage of those fans see our carefully crafted status updates.**

A report from Pagelever (fresh out of beta, and the best Facebook analytics package available, by far) studying 400 million fans found that just 7.49% of fans (on average) see the status updates from any particular brand. This is because of Facebook's EdgeRank algorithm that sanitizes your news feed based on you and your friends' propensity to interact with status updates from each brand and person to whom you're connected on the platform.

Using our email analogy then, we can say that on average (your results may vary), the "open rate" for Facebook is 7.49%, and the "click-through rate" (the interaction rate shown in Insights) mostly ranges from .25% to .9%. Much, much lower than even a middling email campaign.

I'm thinking you'd see a lot less crowing about your 50,000 Facebook likes if you had to report and talk about it using unsexy but true numbers: "3,750 active Facebook likes."

5. Play Your Own Game

Despite the gold rush, social media is still a nascent industry. **One symptom of immature markets is an overwhelming fear of doing it wrong.** Nobody wants to lose their job as CMO of a

major company because of some newfangled medium that didn't exist five minutes ago.

This creates a culture of comparison, whereby instead of spending the requisite time and effort crafting a bespoke social media strategy that uniquely fits our company and its culture, we instead yearn to do it just like the other guys.

Share of voice. Comparisons of twitter followers, Facebook likes, and YouTube subscribers. An over reliance on case studies. Even social media competitor audits(and I do many of them). All of these are byproducts of our collective fear about playing our own game.

Should you learn from your competitors and other companies "doing it right" in social media? Sure, but don't lie to yourself. Realize that **the numbers we proudly toss around like silk sashes are often fictitious hair shirts**. Proceed accordingly. And with caution.

Source: Jay Baer, "5 Reasons Social Media Measurement Is Making You Lie to Yourself." http://www.convinceandconvert.com/social-media-measurement/5-reasons-social-media-measurement-is-making-you-lie-to-yourself/. Used with permission.

So now I don't really hate Newt. It's more that I hate Jay actually. That guy is smarter than I am, and he made me think.

Social media is a really tough place to start building anything. As Jay said, the numbers are public. Whether they should be or not, the numbers are a huge part of how we measure influence online. The thing is, you can't fake the true value that comes from an organically built, engaged following.

When you start out online, focus on sharing solid content, engaging with great people, and being your awesome self. Although it may take a while, you will create your own community, where size is irrelevant.

36

Airline UnAwesome

When you ask for people to share experiences with your brand online, you are going to get feedback, and there is no guarantee you will like what you hear.

NOTHING SAYS MOBILE on-the-go venting in real time quite like air travel. Everywhere you go during travel, people are online and on their phones. Some airlines do an incredible job of online engagement and customer service (i.e., Southwest and WestJet), while others treat it as a broadcast medium only. Worst of all, which brings us to our Hall of Shame nominees, some airlines seem to think that because social media is the platform, regular rules for marketing and customer service don't apply.

Take for example, Spirit Airlines, a US-based carrier who decided to use Twitter as a channel to share sales and promotions online. Unfortunately for the company, they tweeted out these sales without disclosing taxes and fees. They also forgot to include some important details, such as the prices were based on round-trip bookings only.

Because they provided misinformation to customers, they were fined $50,000 by the US Department of Transportation for violating federal rules prohibiting deceptive price advertising.[1]

Just because tweets are only 140 characters that doesn't change the fact that all the other rules and regulations still apply. As businesses, we need to be cautious when sharing promotions online to ensure that they are not misleading and provide followers with all the important information required.

Running community-based contests is a wonderful tool if done properly—and a plane wreck when not.[2]

When our second airline offender, Qantas, decided to run a contest online (see Figure 36.1), they had a few strikes against them right from the start.

QantasAirways Qantas Airways
To enter tell us 'What is your dream luxury inflight experience? (Be creative!) Answer must include #QantasLuxury.TCs qantas.com.au/travel/airline…
3 hours ago

QantasAirways Qantas Airways
Ever wanted to experience Qantas First Class luxury? You could win a First Class gift pack feat. a luxury amenity kit and our famous QF PJs.
3 hours ago

Figure 36.1 Quantus Tweets

For one thing, the timing of the contest could not have been worse, as the airline was in the middle of labor stoppages that were grounding flights, leaving customers stranded and delayed.

Qantas ran a contest using the hashtag #QantasLuxury asking for followers to tweet their luxury in-flight experience for the chance to win a prize of some pajamas. The prize was lame and certainly not fancy enough to keep people from using the hashtag to complain about the brand. The contest totally backfired. The hashtag was hijacked by dissatisfied customers, who shared their negative experiences and horror stories with the brand, not exactly the luxury reviews the company was hoping for. When you clicked the hashtag, or the brand name, mostly all you saw were complaints and bitterness.

---

[1]http://bit.ly/SpiritUnAwesome.
[2]See what I did there? Well, if not, you will in just a second.

One of the reasons brands conduct Twitter contests with a hashtag is that it makes the term easily searchable. So the plan here was for people to tweet their luxury experiences, and when someone else saw the tweet, that person could click the hashtag and see all these awesome Qantas experiences, creating "buzz" and "viralness." Well, apparently offering pajamas to the winner was not enough incentive for people to ignore their negative experiences.

The moral of the story here is that Twitter doesn't fix things; it just makes things louder. You can't choose what people will talk about. And if you add a brand hashtag, be prepared for people to hijack it. When you ask for people to share experiences with your brand online, you are going to get feedback, and there is no guarantee you will like what you hear.

And now for the last of the three musketeers of social airline faux pas, Virgin Airlines. Using sponsored tweets can be an effective way of inserting advertising into popular topics. However, when the system first launched, they probably needed to tweak their filters a little bit, as we can see in Figure 36.2, which shows a collection of tweets about a small plane crash in Toronto.

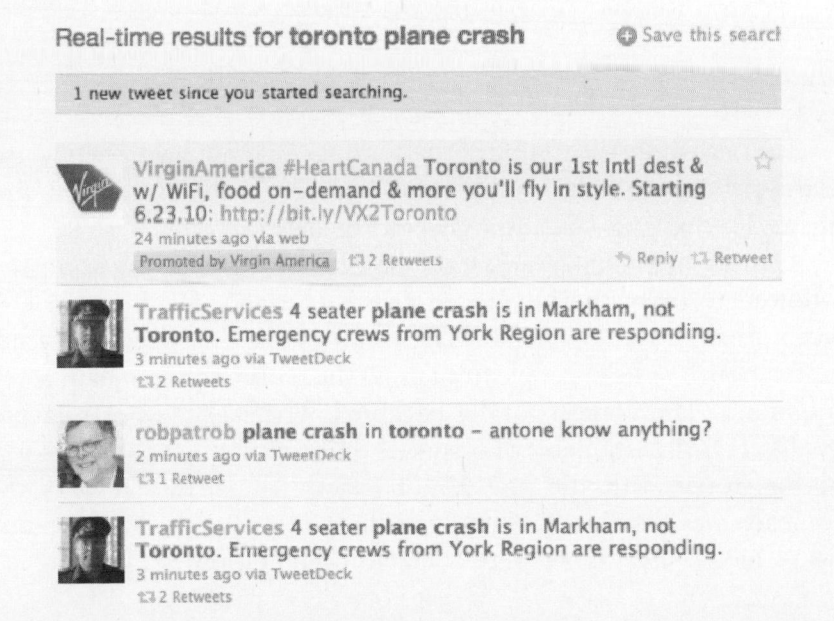

Real-time results for **toronto plane crash**   ⊕ Save this search

1 new tweet since you started searching.

VirginAmerica #HeartCanada Toronto is our 1st Intl dest & w/ WiFi, food on-demand & more you'll fly in style. Starting 6.23.10: http://bit.ly/VX2Toronto
24 minutes ago via web
Promoted by Virgin America   ↻ 2 Retweets   ↻ Reply ↻ Retweet

TrafficServices 4 seater **plane crash** is in Markham, not **Toronto**. Emergency crews from York Region are responding.
3 minutes ago via TweetDeck
↻ 2 Retweets

robpatrob **plane crash** in **toronto** – antone know anything?
2 minutes ago via TweetDeck
↻ 1 Retweet

TrafficServices 4 seater **plane crash** is in Markham, not **Toronto**. Emergency crews from York Region are responding.
3 minutes ago via TweetDeck
↻ 2 Retweets

Figure 36.2   Virgin Sponsored Tweet

I'm going to go ahead and say that it looks to me like airplane crashes are sponsored by Virgin. Contextual advertising is a breakthrough for the industry on platforms like Google, Facebook, and even Twitter. But you've got to make sure the context is correct and not just keyword based. I can't think of a worse context to have your airline ad appear than in news about a crash.

All of these stories came from big companies, with big budgets to do awesome things online. But nothing compares to the outrage of geeks online. No budget can outspend them, no mute button can silence them, and no apology can outfly them.

37

Political UnAwesome

Because they are elected by the public, politicians already live in a very public sphere, and they need to be accountable for the things they say, both online and offline.

NOTHING SAYS APPROPRIATE and transparent quite like politicians. And by that, I sarcastically mean they are often online train wrecks. For the most part, politicians are the reason media filters exist. Well-crafted speeches, spins, and puppeteering don't exactly scream Twitter out the gate. And this has led to some incredibly awesome, horrific experiences online, that all really helped show what the politicians involved were "made of."

These nominees for the Hall of Shame demonstrate all the aspects of UnAwesome we spoke about in the introduction. Because they are elected by the public, politicians already live in a very public sphere, and they need to be accountable for the things they say, both online and offline. Social media amplifies this for good and for bad. In general I really don't believe this is a bad thing. Although the politicians here

may have made Hall of Shame quality mistakes, aren't we all better off knowing their true colors so that we can make more educated choices?

After meeting Kansas Senator Samuel Brownback on a field trip, Emma Sullivan, a high school student, did what many of us do on social media and shared her opinion about a public figure. She tweeted that he "#blowsalot."

Not really anything to see here, right? Just move along.

But that's not what happened.

It would seem that the teen and her comment touched a nerve. The governor decided that Emma's tweeting was out of line and needed to be stopped. He chose to call up her high school principal and complain. Emma was given a good talking to and ordered to write a letter of apology.

Instead, Emma refused and announced on Twitter that she would not be sending any sorry letters and would not take back her original tweet (see Figure 37.1).

Figure 37.1   Tweet from @emmakate988

If you want to turn the public against you, just try censoring them. Getting a teenager to be quiet about anything as a parent is hard enough. Requesting a tweet or post to be taken down, treating the opinionated teenager like an outspoken employee, that's a huge mistake.

Emma's original tweet was fairly harmless and could not possibly have been seen as a threat to the senator's career or standing with the public. When she tweeted it, she had only 60 followers[1] (she now has more than 14,000). All this did was make him look like the inexperienced youth and her look like she should be running for state congress.

---

[1] http://bit.ly/TeenUnApology.

The senator did end up apologizing to Emma and agreed the response was definitely an overreaction, stating:

> My staff over-reacted to this tweet, and for that I apologize. Freedom of speech is among our most treasured freedoms. I enjoyed speaking to the more than 100 students who participated in the Youth in Government Program at the Kansas Capitol. They are our future. I also want to thank the thousands of Kansas educators who remind us daily of our liberties, as well as the values of civility and decorum. Again, I apologize for our over-reaction.

What I love most about this story is that the teen reminded the senator about the importance of freedom of speech. He may be a part of the Hall of Shame, but I think Emma and how she stood her ground and taught him a lesson is all kinds of awesome.

Next in line, for our politician of the year award, we have Republican New Jersey candidate Phil Mitsch, who learned the lesson of off-color jokes and how your inside-the-head voice needs to stay inside your thick head. After gaining more than 44,000 followers, he decided to expand his professional field to include women counseling, with this hearty piece of advice to his then 44,000 followers.

> Women, you increase your odds of keeping your men by being faithful, a lady in the living room and a whore in the bedroom.

He did end up apologizing, saying he meant it as a joke. The problem with apologizing is that it never catches up to the original incident. And I'm not sure what he's apologizing for here; he's showing his true self, which I think helps everybody, because they can now make their own judgment without filters. This particular case just doesn't work out too well for him, but he should have thought of that before tweeting.

Next on our list is the infamous Senator Anthony Weiner. It's the kind of thing late night television show hosts dream of: a politician with a phallic name tweeting a picture of his junk. We've all been there, right? No? Really? Put yourself in his shoes. What would you do if this happened to you? I personally would return all electronics, move to the mountains, and learn how to eat berries. He chose the

route of saying he had been hacked, which is code for I have farked up big time and now I'm panicking.

In this situation saying you have been hacked is like taking your TV out of your living room and saying you've been robbed. Sure enough, it came in the press that not only was it a picture of his cash and prizes but that he was having an affair; he ended up resigning his political position.

A similar situation amazingly enough happened here in Canada to one of our "members"[2] of parliament when he sent out a picture of his thankfully underwear-covered "package" and said his phone went off in his pants. His pants must have some great lighting.

So there you have it: political UnAwesome at its best. The moral of the story is that it takes a thousand tweets to build your reputation and one politician to ruin it.

---

[2] Tee hee.

38

Chrysler

It takes 1,000 tweets to build your reputation and one to ruin it.

THE AUTOMOTIVE HALL of Shame nominee comes to us with a lesson about using a program that allows you to tweet from multiple accounts. Although it is beneficial to easily switch from one account to another, it can also be very dangerous if the lines get crossed, as you can see from the tweet shown in Figure 38.1.

Scott Bartosiewicz was having a frustrating commute to work and decided to tweet the fact. And then he clicked Update. Unfortunately for Scott, the company he worked for, New Media Strategies, ran Chrysler's Twitter account and Scott was the person in charge of it. As you can probably notice from the figure, the tweet was mistakenly sent out from Chrysler's account.[1]

To say that Scott probably should have thought twice about the tweet would be taking it easy on him. Even if the tweet had come up

---

[1]http://bit.ly/ChryslerUnAwesome.

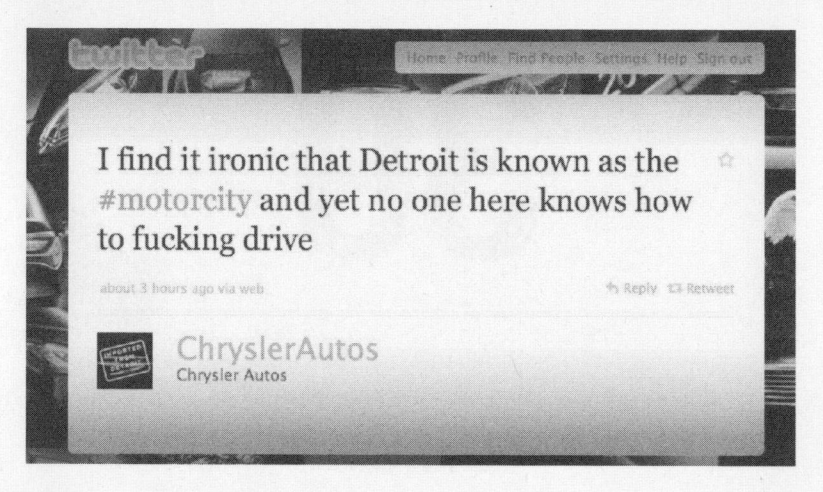

Figure 38.1   Tweet from @ChryslerAutos

only on his personal account, his connection to the car company, in a city known for the automotive industry, made it pretty risky to begin with. The fact that he was managing Chrysler's account and expected to be an expert in social media made it a whole lot riskier, and less forgivable.

This all happened shortly after Chrysler spent a truckload of money on a new Super Bowl campaign showing their Detroit pride, with the new tagline "Imported from Detroit." This tweet could do more to damage that campaign than any paid appearance by Eminem could fix.

The tweet was deleted. The standard apology tweet of "Our account has been compromised" was sent. Scott was fired. And Chrysler did not renew their services contract with New Media Strategies—all because of an emotional, reactionary tweet from someone who should have known better.

People accuse me of being overly dramatic when I say it takes 1,000 tweets to build your reputation and one to ruin it; I think they're wrong, and Detroit would agree with me.

For a cool comparison, you can check out the Red Cross story over on the *Awesome* side (Chapter 38), to see a similar mistake that resulted from an account mix-up but that was not only fixed but created a window for awesome.

39

Dilbert

Never meet your heroes.

SOMETIMES AUTHENTICITY AND TRANSPARENCY are not a good thing, especially if you're a meathead. There's a great line that says "Never meet your heroes." In this day and age, not only can we meet them, but we can talk with them. And this interaction can change the way you think about their brand... instantly.

For the past 20 years, two comic strips have really helped me hone my sarcastic and witty communication style. *The Far Side* and *Dilbert* are my bibles of the crass world. *The Far Side* cartoon of the kid pushing on the door marked "Pull" at the "Midvale School for the Gifted" is a poster for my entire generation. With *Dilbert*, I was that guy. I had the desk calendar, all the anthologies, and even the Dogbert hardcover books about business. To say I was a fan boy would be an understatement.

Today, I am no longer a fan. I started learning about *Dilbert*'s creator Scott Adams, not because I went looking for information

about him, but because he started talking, when he really should have just kept drawing. Turns out, he's a real prick.

For one, he created an online pseudonym to fight critics, spending months pretending to be his own greatest fan just so he could attack people saying negative things about him or his work on message boards. The whole thing began on a thread talking about an article Adams had written about himself for the *Wall Street Journal*. In the article, he talked about how brilliant and successful he was, even though he didn't "get straight A's" in school. The thread began getting a ton of negative comments, calling Adams out as an egomaniac. Rather than defend himself, or have real fans come to his aid, an account called PlannedChaos stepped in. PlannedChaos viciously defended Adams.

After a while, a few of the MetaFilter users called the account out and Adams confessed that it was him, saying, "I am Scott Adams." Then he said good-bye: "I'm sorry I peed in your cesspool."

He also spoke up about men's rights and his belief that men suffer "a level of social injustice equal to women" and then he said this . . .

> The reality is that women are treated differently by society for exactly the same reason that children and the mentally handicapped are treated differently. It's just easier this way for everyone. You don't argue with a four-year old about why he shouldn't eat candy for dinner. You don't punch a mentally handicapped guy even if he punches you first. And you don't argue when a women tells you she's only making 80 cents to your dollar. It's the path of least resistance. You save your energy for more important battles.[1]

It is safe to say my view of him has changed. I can't even read a *Dilbert* comic strip without thinking about these kinds of things. Now some people say there is no such thing as bad publicity, but I think they are the same people who like cold calling and tell their kids to suck it up every time they get hurt. Because of his words and his views, I will never again buy another *Dilbert* product—which just leaves me more room for more *Far Side* stuff.

---

[1] http://aol.it/DilbertUnAwesome.

40

The UnAwesome End

This side of the book isn't about companies behaving badly; this is about companies having bad people.

I CONSIDERED EACH ONE OF THE HALL of Shame nominees, trying to pick the "winner," and I just couldn't do it. There are really no winners here. Each is a worst-case scenario of how to behave in business and online. These crimes committed here are beyond a PR rescue, in a space where no viral video or rebranding campaign can help them. Social media cannot fix your product, your employees, or your values. It simply amplifies your mistakes.

We all love a good train wreck, and there are as many lessons to be learned from the best as there are from the worst. Think twice before you tweet, remember be respectful and kind, and never forget that when you are online, you are in public—and the things you say will be held against you, and your company, in the court of public opinion.

This side of the book isn't about companies behaving badly; this is about companies having bad people. It's the individual people who

126

earned companies' entrance to the UnAwesome Hall of Shame; it was never about their product or service. If you want to be better, hire better. And if you don't consider this a warning, I have a third book to write and I'm dying for content.

If you started the book here and are headed over to the Awesome side, get your glass half-full ready and enjoy the rarely seen great side of business. Don't you worry; I will be here waiting bitterly for you when you're done.

If you started this journey on the Awesome side, you're now at the end, but really it's just the beginning. Come on over to TheBookOf -BusinessUnAwesome.com for updates and new stories and to share your own. You can shoot me an e-mail right now to unawesome@ un-marketing.com, or send me a tweet at @unmarketing to share your stories.